Cumbrian
Women Remember

Lake District Life in the Early 1900s

JUNE THISTLETHWAITE

Thyme Press

To four favourite Cumbrian men –
one supportive husband and three sons

Other books in this series:
'Cumbria the War Years' 1997
'Molly's Story' 1998
'Excused Boots' 1999

Published by Thyme Press, 5 Finley Close,
Kendal, Cumbria LA9 6DW

First Published 1995
First Reprint 1995
Second Reprint 1997
Third Reprint 1998
Fourth Reprint 2000

Designed by Linda Blakemore
Printed by Kent Valley Colour Printers Ltd, Kendal

British Library Cataloguing in Publication Data
A Catalogue record for this book is available from the British Library
ISBN 0 9531695 0 2

Contents

Acknowledgements

I am grateful to the families of the late Annie Dawson and Mary Hayhurst for allowing me to include their mothers' stories. The help I have received from both families has been very much appreciated.

Mr J. Grisenthwaite (County Archivist), Mrs Ethel Fisher (Seaton) and Mrs S. Gosling (Kendal) all provided valuable advice, and Shambles Antiques (Kendal) loaned some of the items used for the cover photograph. I would also like to thank K.T.D. Office Equipment Ltd, Tyre Services G.B. and Kentdale Studio (Kendal) for their help.

Most of the photographs in the book are reproduced courtesy of the interviewees but I am also indebted to the following for pictures which appear on the pages listed: The Cumbria Police Museum for p. 183; Mr G. Dawson for pp. 11, 14, 77, 78, 172 and 173; A. Fraser (Penrith) for p. 92; Mrs I. Jackson (Kendal) for p. 61; Jennings Brothers PLC for p. 179; Lindsay's Butchers (Cockermouth) for p. 186; N. Watson (Penrith) for p. 158; Ms F. Walker (Kendal) for p. 76; the *Westmorland Gazette* for p. 95 (below); Mr Woodruff (Workington) for pp. 46, 48, 68, 69, 70, 141 and 144. Whilst every effort has been made to trace all copyright holders, I apologise to any holders not acknowledged, and would be grateful to be notified of any corrections to be incorporated in future editions.

Finally, without the acceptance of one very basic chapter, followed by their guidance and help, this book would still be only jottings on a note pad. Therefore, the biggest thank you to Kelly and Ian at Ellenbank Press.

Cumbria

SCOTLAND

NORTHUMBERLAND

● Brampton

● CARLISLE

● Wigton

Alston

● Aspatria
Allonby
● Maryport
● Flimby ● Cockermouth
● Seaton
Workington
● Harrington
Lorton
● Keswick

● Penrith

DURHAM

Kings Meaburn
● Appleby

Glenridding
● Whitehaven
Rowrah
● Buttermere
● Martindale
● Shap

● Brough

● Kirkby Stephen

● Kentmere
● Ambleside
Ravenstonedale

● Ravenglass
● Staveley
Windermere
● Kendal ● Sedbergh

NORTH
YORKSHIRE

Ulverston
Kirkby Lonsdale

Grange-
over-Sands

Barrow

LANCASHIRE

Introduction

'I can remember when the *Titanic* went down. I was living at Workington at the time and our neighbours dashed in to tell us the news.' This chance remark by a neighbour made me think. I know so little about the lives of people who live in our county or even locally. All too often when someone dies, a snippet of their past is uncovered. A chance remark is made or a keepsake found of some sentimental value. Almost guiltily we say, 'I didn't know about that. Why didn't they mention it?' The opportunity has gone.

We have information about steel-workers, bobbin-makers and those involved in other male industries but very little about the women behind the scenes – those who put the house in order, bore the children and watched the pennies. The one Cumbrian woman we have all heard of is Dorothy Wordsworth. But would we have heard of William if Dorothy hadn't been prepared to make his meals and look after him?

The following lives give us a glimpse of a time soon to be forgotten. This century has brought so many changes so quickly that it is often hard to recognise the recent past. As Rita commented wryly when reflecting on her life, 'I don't even sound as though I'm from Dickens' time, more like Shakespeare's.' With this in mind, I have let the women speak for themselves. As far as possible I've used their own words and expressions.

The one phrase they all kept repeating was '. . . and that was that.' There was no need for further explanation. It was finished, the end. This remark was made when speaking about leaving school, looking after aged parents or some other event beyond their control. These women simply got on with life. Again, the war years were taken in their stride. Yes there were bombings, yes it was frightening. It was acknowledged as a difficult time '. . . and that was that'.

They had all experienced hard times but none of them spoke about this with bitterness. It was a fact of life. Money was scarce, Father was strict, Mother coped and everyone worked. Humour was essential and this sparkled through every conversation.

Similar characteristics emerged among all the ladies – active, open minds, humour, common sense and frankness. A very good combination. Although their stories may add to our knowledge of the past, they certainly weren't collected for academic analysis. In true Cumbrian tradition, they were obtained as the result of 'a good crack and natter' and purely for enjoyment.

How did I start on this project? Armed only with enthusiasm and a tape-recorder. First I listened to neighbours and then someone would say, 'Oh, you should talk to my husband's aunt' or 'Go and see my mother's cousin, she can tell you some tales,' and it led on from there. Also, the clergy gave invaluable help by recommending ladies in their parishes.

I was nervous and so were the interviewees, many of whom expressed doubt as to the interest of their lives. Ann at Glenridding had been worried that I might be posh. When she realised I had the same accent as herself, it was 'Ee, lass that's grand. Shall I get the bottle [wine] out?' Unfortunately I had to decline. But no one was dull, everyone had a story to tell.

Through these conversations I realised the part the Women's Institute and church played and still plays in the lives of so many people, especially in rural districts; also the importance of the railways in the life of the county. Such poverty accepted with humour and such close-knit families. And now, so many mines, industries, farms and communities have gone.

What remains? Cumbria is a big county, both in size and in heart. Wherever I went, there was always a cup of tea ready. Everyone was kind, from the interviewees to strangers I rang with questions. People went out of their way to be helpful. It surprised me that, even as strangers, we all knew each other. We all had friends, relations or a mutual sympathy in common, no matter what our backgrounds.

Amongst the ladies I interviewed, there was no snobbishness. Everyone considered themselves to be working class, for they had worked hard throughout their lives. Achievements were played down or even brushed aside. All had different personalities but were united by the fact that they had always given of themselves and got on with the job in hand . . . and that was that.

'It was seven days a week was farming'

HANNAH BRACKEN (b. 1910)
Sedbergh/Garsdale

My dad was born and lived out Kettle way. Then he went shepherding to Bar Gap and married when he was there. I was born at Bar Gap in 1910 but shortly after we moved up Shap Abbey way, to a place called Mosedale, and I left there when I was five. I went for a holiday to an aunt and uncle of my mother's at Sleatham and they kept me. You see, they hadn't any family of their own and they wanted me there. It wasn't unusual in those days. You would often hear of children living with other relations. My sister was brought up at home but, as this aunt and uncle wanted me, my parents let me stay with them. It didn't really bother me but I didn't see my mam and dad very much – it might be months before we met up.

This aunt and uncle, who I called 'Granny' and 'Granda', already had a grown-up niece living with them on the farm and she did the housekeeping. They had a big farm and a lot of sheep but the snow-storms were terrific in them days and it was a problem sometimes, getting the sheep down off the fells when the storms came. Granda had to go with a horse and sledge and make tracks in the snow for the sheep to follow. In winter a lot of wagonloads of hay came to Bowes on the railway and Granda would collect it, bringing it by horse and cart up to the farm. That railway was a lifeline but now they've done away with it and it's all lorries. For market we went by horse and trap to Barney [Barnard] Castle (eight miles away). 'Barney' was quite a big place, with a market in the centre of the road where folk used to go and sell their produce.

I started at Bowes School, which was four miles away, when I was five or six. I either had to walk two miles across the fell to the school bus or, when I was old enough, I could cycle the four miles. There wasn't any kiddies lived right near to me but I might join up with some more before I got to the school road. Sometimes, during winter, Granny and me came down to Bowes and stayed in a cottage that she had. Then I only had to walk across the road to school and that was grand. I can't tell you

9

anything about the cottage now – only that it was opposite Bowes School and I went to Bowes Sunday School from there. They were both handy, you see. Otherwise a lot of the time in winter I never got to school.

I used to take jam sandwiches and cold tea to school. There was no hot dinners in them days and we supped the tea cold. Bowes School was quite big with a lot of kiddies and we used slates and blue pencils. Gordon Hitchcock was the head teacher and I was always frightened of him because he was a bit sharp with us. I wasn't the best of scholars, as I didn't get to school when I should have done on account of the weather. It was only when we were in the cottage at Bowes that I managed to get to Sunday School. But wherever we were, we never did anything on a Sunday except what we were forced to do.

We went to school in clogs and cut the feet off old ribbed stockings, making gaiters out of them, to put over the clogs to keep the snow out. There was no Wellingtons then but they were a boon when we did get them. I still like my Wellingtons best of owt to keep my legs warm. I wore a jumper, skirt and pinafore but we had a smock for milking and doing among the cows. You know, we had some wild weather. I've known it rain for weeks and we hardly had a dry coat about the spot. There wasn't the waterproofs like there are today.

I hadn't anybody to play with in the evening. When I came back from school I worked on the farm among the stock, as there was the cows to water, sheep to feed and suchlike. There was a couple of men working on the farm who lodged there, and we'd have our meals together in the kitchen. As Granny was getting on in years, we didn't play cards. It was just doing some knitting, sewing or playing dominoes. There was no visiting relations or anything like that. When you were done on a night, you were ready for bed. There was no electric, wireless, television or anything like that. No, it was bed, and you were stuck with a paraffin lamp or a candle. It was a big farmhouse and I had an old-fashioned stone hot water bottle for bedtime as it could be awfully cold.

I had a pillowcase at Christmas and got presents off Granny and Mam and Dad. I'd get toffees, fruit, chocolate and maybe some clothes. If you were naughty, you got cinders in the pillowcase, which I did occasionally. I remember I was about thirteen when I found out there wasn't a Father Christmas and I got the shock of my life.

By this time my own family were living at Fell End and I went back to live with them when I was thirteen. Grandma had died and it wasn't the same after she'd gone. While I was home on holiday, Granda was killed. He was taking some sheep over to Brough and got out of the wagon to see if they were all right and a car ran into him. So I never went back to the farm or to Bowes School. You see, in them days I don't think they could force you to go to school when you were nearly fourteen. I stayed at home for a bit. Then I went to work at Narthwaite, to a house that took in visitors. I was only there six months because they were going to get another girl to help me. Well, they never did and I cleaned, washed up and cooked, getting up at six o'clock, and I wouldn't finish until night. It was all go, with the washing for the visitors, and I had to work hard. There wasn't a half-day or a weekend off. You worked every day.

After that I went into farm service near Sedbergh. I was paid £20 for six months and I was thought to have a big wage. I used to do the milking and the milk round, so the boss bought me extra waterproofs. I hadn't been hired to go on the milk round but I suppose they were short of staff. When I eventually left that place the next girl only got £13 for six months. The boss dursn't ask her if she would do the milking at that price.

Every morning I got up about half-past five and the first thing would be to get breakfast, help milk the cows and get away with the milk. It was quite a big milk round and covered a lot of Sedbergh and some of the big schools. The boss and me went out in the pony and trap with the tin cans and tiny cream cans and left a can of milk on everybody's doorstep. When we came back to the farm I carried on with the housework. One farm lad was kept to help out, as there would be about sixteen cows milking and possibly some would be in calf or on the way, as well as sheep and horses.

Sedbergh

We finished work at about six o'clock, in time for supper, and after that you could do what you liked – go out or stay in. I used to go out a bit, usually to some Chapel 'do' or something like that. I was never one for going to dances or the pictures or that sort of thing. Generally there was a social evening, with someone talking or singing.

I worked at Christmas. It was seven days a week was farming and the milk round, and people wanted their milk every day. I usually got tips at that time of the year. Lambing time and haytime would be the busiest times on the farm and, as we were hired for six months, we got a fortnight's holiday a year. Then I'd go home to my parents as a rule, taking a friend with me.

I met my husband at a social 'do' and married when I was twenty. He was from Garsdale way, although his parents had been down in Liverpool for a while, selling milk, before they returned to farming. There had been thirteen in their family, but they lost three. One of them was killed in the First World War. They never knew what happened to him.

Oh the 'old fella' [father-in-law] was a character. He never used to speak if the family was making a noise – he would just hit them with his knuckles – and they knew when they had to behave. I was frightened of my father, although I was never really at home. Same with the old fella – they were all frightened of him. I've often wondered how in the name of goodness my mother-in-law coped, doing her own baking and all that lot to feed. Men didn't do anything in the house. It's different today.

We got married at Garsdale Church and I wore a brown dress and hat. There wasn't any great posh robes in them days. My reception was at my sister-in-law's at Garsdale village. For our honeymoon, we went down to Liverpool. Well, I'd never been in a town like that before. It was all strange to me. We went out and about and to the shops and I managed to get from one place to another on the buses.

Our first house was just a tiny cottage above Garsdale village; it's been taken down now. It was only one room to live in and there was a scullery at the back. Then upstairs there'd be just one bedroom and a box room. It was very tiny. The toilet was outside and there was no water in the house – I had to go across the road to the farm for that. We were there about eighteen months before we moved to a bigger house about half a mile from the main road. But again, there was no inside toilet or water. We got the water across the yard from a spring that ran into a trough. Oh, you had all your water to carry and there was no bathroom, only tin baths. We still had paraffin lamps and candles for lighting and a fireside oven for cooking. Eventually we got one of those paraffin ovens, which was easier because you just put it on when you wanted to use it. I often wonder how we managed.

I had all my family at home and all the nappies to wash by hand. You had a big round boiler in the wash house and had to light a coal fire to heat the water before you could boil clothes. In those days you never bothered seeing a doctor when you were expecting, not until a week or two before the baby was born. There wasn't the carry-on there is today, going for tests and scans. The doctor would come for the birth and a local lady did the midwifing, but that was all the help I had. One of my babies was only six months old when we both caught measles and were in bed. Both my sisters-in-law came to help out then.

My husband was working on a farm at the time or doing a bit of walling – he found work where he could. Sometimes he would go to Kentmere Hall near Kendal to catch rabbits, going on Monday morning and coming back on Saturday night. He went by pushbike – that was the only way of getting there – and stayed with a man called Teddy Hanley and his wife who was working at the Hall. Oh they worked forever during the day and used to go round with a horse and pick the rabbits up at night, stringing them over the horse to get them all in. I suppose they sold them at shops somewhere to make a bit of money.

We only had a bit of garden either side of the house door but we had upward of 400 hens and I looked after a lot of them. We had proper incubators and people used to bring me batches of their eggs to hatch out. In them days we sold the eggs to hatcheries, one at Hebden Bridge and one near Skipton. The eggs that didn't go to a hatchery went to Pratt's at Sedbergh. Well, in summer I got ninepence a dozen for the eating eggs. But for our hatching eggs, they paid for fertility and I got seven shillings and sixpence a dozen. Pratt's had two wagonloads of eggs from down in Garsdale every Tuesday, because everybody had eggs. We had a car by then, to take the eggs to Sedbergh. We were one of the first to get a car in Garsdale and paid thirty something pound for it. It was a Morris 8 that we got off our landlord.

There wasn't a lot of socialising in them days. At Christmas we'd go to a few do's. One was at the little chapel in 'the street' [Garsdale village], one at Garsdale Foot Chapel and then there was the social at Sedbergh Methodist Chapel. There would be some dances but I never went. Well, you had plenty on at home, but if you wanted to go you'd get onto the pushbike and go. People made their own entertainment and would go round to neighbours in winter for a night out, sitting and playing dominoes. Same as we did, going to our next-door neighbour, having supper and a right chat.

There would be the odd break-in here and there but not the big quantity there is today. Going way back, a relation of my husband's who farmed up the Cautley Road heard somebody in the house one night. He

Sedbergh, Cautley Crags

went downstairs and found this man. This relation was only in his shirtsleeves but walked the burglar to the police station at Sedbergh. Then he said to the policeman, 'I'll have to get back home because the wife will wonder where I's at.' He had some pluck, hadn't he? They said the burglar thought there'd be money in the house because this relation had sold a cow that day at Sedbergh auction.

About six years later we moved by horse and cart to another farm that had about 137 acres. Oh I didn't like it when I came into Garsdale – I didn't like it a bit. In our previous house we got the sun whenever it came out, but we came here in February and there was a lot of snow and we didn't see the sun for weeks. When you moved to a farm you bought your own sheep unless you took them over from the previous tenant. You see, some farms were let on condition that you took the sheep over. We bought our own stock and I know the first two cows we sold made £27.10 shillings each. That wasn't much, was it? When we sold our draft ewes in the back end, we might get £7. If we got £7.10 shillings it was thought to be a good price. At that time, two or three farmers joined together and walked the lambs to market but we always hired a wagon for the cattle.

We rented the farm when we first moved here and I think 11th November and 12th May were the rent days. The landlord lived at Hawes Junction and my husband would have to go up and pay until we bought the farm a few years later. We rented pasture land and an allotment (that's the land belonging to a farm that goes right up on the tops) from a relation who lived near. We had shorthorn cows, pigs and sheep.

The hen house, which took up the whole top left-hand side of the building

I still had my incubators and got far more for eggs than they do today. It's all so dear now and then these restrictions came and that Edwina Currie – I could have kicked her backside! It was her that did me with the eggs, you see. They had to be tested and everything. Well, I had to give over because it was costing so much to have the eggs tested. It was all wrong. There hadn't been any trouble before that.

I had hens right up the pastures and we didn't fasten them in at night because they were never touched by foxes. There didn't seem to be as many foxes as now. This lambing time folk have lost a lot of lambs already. It's a bit of a rum 'un really as they're old foxes and can dodge the hounds. They can go through the river or anywhere to make the hounds lose their scent. Then they get into their holes and won't bolt and in a lot of places they daren't put the terriers in. Years ago, if anything was stirring my husband and his mates would be after them.

We always had a good dog or two. A lot of them didn't take much training. They would more or less train themselves if you had a good breed. I could go out and send the dogs right round by that skyline, just as my husband could. I always liked what they called an 'eye' dog. Some dogs set [sit and stare at the sheep] too much because the sheep stop with an 'eye' dog. It'll set and not shift the sheep, you see.

Haytime was the busiest time of year. You were dependent on the weather and there was everything to do with the rake. We had some rough times, I can tell you. I did a lot of mowing, getting up at half-past three in the morning to do that with the horse and machine. You had to get it done before it got hot in them days. No wonder my legs are bad, walking miles and miles and putting in up to eighteen hours a day. We didn't have time to make hot dinners or owt. I know my husband was annoyed once when we were nearly finished haytiming. He said, 'Now, you can do what you like as soon as you've finished making dinner.' Well, if it didn't blooming well go and rain by the time I was getting dinner made . . . I think it was about a month before we got that bit of hay in. If we'd carried on we'd have got it in. But we didn't, we stopped for something to eat. Neighbours had their own work to do but if anyone got finished they would help you out. We all helped one another.

We also had eight sows, so there was always plenty of work. These were sold to a firm at Chorley, and Wilson's wagon from Endmoor used to collect them and take them there. We always kept a pig for ourselves, and a local butcher would come and butch it for us. You always had your own pig butched at home but now, of course, you can't do that. You never get the bacon these days same as what we used to produce and kill ourselves. We killed a big pig and kept the ham for haytime. Many a time the pigs would be up to thirty-two stone – great fat pigs they were. The fatter they were, the better we liked them. We got all our fat for baking and we had some lovely home-cured bacon. I used to make as many tins of black pudding as possible. Our lads were nobbut saying the other day, 'By gum, but Mother's black puddings would be good today.' You know, the more you ate them, the better you seemed to like them.

We had our own engine – a little Dales engine – for light, wireless and to run the milking machine, as it wasn't until 1961 that we got electricity. Farming isn't the same today, with all this form-filling. Well, there was the agricultural returns once a year and you filled them in, putting down what stock was on the farm. That was it, you'd finished. Not like today.

I still went to church socials and every Wednesday was the farmers' half-day. That's when we all went to Sedbergh and there was the auction. It was in the main street in those days, where the car park is now. So farmers did their shopping on that day and then went to the auction. Sedbergh has changed. Same as the Dales. There's a lot of fresh people come in. There was five or six grocery shops in Sedbergh when I used to go shopping. But I never went on holiday save once when I went down to Liverpool to see my relations.

I liked a good agricultural show. We went to Kendal, Kirkby Lonsdale and Appleby because my brother-in-law was very keen on showing shepherds' crooks. My husband liked to dress sticks that he made himself with hazel and horn and he won prizes with them. He filed them down, then melted them to turn as he wanted, and that took a bit of doing. I loved a show, to meet up with everybody and be among the stock. It was about the only outing we got, you see.

My eldest children went to Garsdale School, which was about a mile and a half away. There was a school taxi, so they were picked up and taken. Then, when they got to eleven, they had to go to Sedbergh for school. But the youngest children went to Sedbergh from five years old, as Garsdale School Room was made into the parish hall.

All my family went to Sunday School and one of them had eleven years of unbroken attendance. They went whatever the weather as they hadn't to break their attendance. There used to be a church and three chapels in the Dale but one has closed now. When my in-laws were alive they went down to Garsdale Foot Chapel on a Sunday morning, then came home and had their dinner. After dinner they walked to Garsdale Street Chapel in the afternoon, came back home, did their work and had their tea, before walking back again to Garsdale Foot for the service at night. And in them days the preachers would walk into Dent and over into Grisedale for the services.

My parents and sister were living at Rentside, up on Stainmore, by this time and still farming. Oh bless my life, yes that was out in the country. They were six miles from Kirkby Stephen and my mother had to walk two miles to Barras Station whenever she went to town to sell her butter and eggs and carry all her shopping. My mother had a rough life and worked hard, with farming and dashing about. She was fifty-nine when she died with cancer and there was nothing they could do in those days. She never told me until the very last and I got a terrific shock because I'd never heard much about cancer. You see, in them days you didn't. After my mother went, Dad moved to a little place near Kirkby Stephen, again as a tenant farmer.

Sedbergh and District Home Guard

The war made a big difference. Everything was blacked out and my husband was in the Home Guard. There was quite a few in the Dale here in the Home Guard and they went maybe one night a week up to the Tank House at Hawes Junction on duty. They would sleep in this Tank House. They weren't supposed to but they did. The men had a fire and a kettle to make themselves a drink and some of them had a lie-down. A bomb dropped beyond Hawes Junction and then there was one out near Selside which we heard. I think my husband went up to High Fields and he could see the reflection of the fire at Selside in the sky. We used to sit and listen for the planes and say, 'Oh, that's Jerry.' We reckoned we knew when Jerry was coming over by the sound of the plane. There was more ploughing to do during the war. As we had our own farm and rented land, we had two haytimes and only one horse. We did get two horses at the finish but it was still to do by hand.

The only way to our farm was over a bridge and that had been built with girders from Hawes Junction. Well, they'd had to saw these girders and join them in the middle with sleepers, one either side of the bridge to hold it up. With the floods of '47, one of these sleepers had been washed away. Then, when the coal lorry came over, the bridge collapsed and the back end of the lorry went into the river. So when straw and hay and everything was being delivered, they had to rig a pulley up and swing it across the river. The bridge was only put back two days before my youngest was born. If I'd wanted the doctor before that . . . well, we were up to our waists in slush and snow . . . I could have gone to Highlands, the nursing home at Sedbergh, but I said, 'Oh, no I'm stopping here.' I didn't realise the danger I was in, you know. But we were never snowed in for long. They had to get the road cut open to get the milk out, you see.

Quite a while since, there was a family on every farm. Up at Grisedale there used to be eight different families, where now there'll only be two. I think people had to go away to make a living and a lot of little farms have been made into big ones. They were all lived in at one time but now there's a lot of holiday cottages. In the Dales you knew everybody and what they were called. Well, now I don't know half of them. Sometimes wagons stop and the drivers say, 'Can you tell me where so and so lives?' I say, 'If you tell me the name of the place, I'll tell you, but I don't know the name of the person.' You see, it was a different way of life here. One woman who's lost her husband, she still does a lot of the farm work and she must be in her seventies. I was talking to her sister recently and asked after this woman. Her sister said, 'Oh, she's among the sheep, doing the lambing.' We don't retire at sixty or sixty-five here, we keep going.

TWO

'We used to call him Lord Lace Holes'

ELSIE BLENKARN (b. 1908)
Shap/Hardendale/Orton/Greenholme

Most of the men at Shap worked at the quarries, either the blue rock or granite, and the main road was closed for a while if there was to be a big explosion. In the village was a Co-op where everybody used to get their dividend. You spent your money and were given a ticket to stick on a sheet. At the year end it was all reckoned up and you could draw your 'divi' out or leave it in. You got quite a nice little bit and thought 'Eh, that's grand.'

Then there was old Ellen Atkinson's sweetshop at the end of Foster Street. I used to go there twice a week and buy a halfpenny-worth of sweets. Groceries were ordered once a month from Hetherington's and Mr Hulse, the shopkeeper, always put a free quarter of toffees in the box for the kiddies.

My parents had moved to Shap before I was born in 1908. Dad was originally from Newby but worked down south before going with his two brothers to Canada. They went right across the Rockies, stole rides on the railroads and did all sorts of jobs. But Dad came back, as he was courting my mother in England.

Mother was from Berkeley in Gloucestershire and started work in service when she was eleven years old. She'd met my dad when he was working at a farm in that area before he went abroad. After they married, they moved to Foster Street at Shap and Dad got a job dry-stone walling for Lowther's. Our house had a loft and Dad made a barrow up there. Unfortunately the barrow was too big and Dad couldn't get it down!

I remember we used to go by Foster's trap from Shap to Penrith to see my grandmother. Foster's trap went to Penrith every Tuesday, as he was the carrier and brought all kinds of stuff back. On Little Whit Tuesday we always visited Grandma and went to the fair. The hirings were on at Whitsuntide but the Tuesday was special for the children. When I had whooping cough I was taken to Penrith Gas Works to smell

Elsie's parents

the gas and get it up my nostrils. I don't know if it did any good but that's what they used to do in those days.

In 1914 Dad took a farm at Hardendale. We moved to Nook Farm on 25th March, which was Lady Day, when all the rents had to be paid. The farmhouse had a living room on the left and a parlour on the right. The stairs leading upstairs were stone steps. Most unusual was the dairy, which had a tap, as we had a well and a spring not far away. The tap sometimes used to dry up in summer and water had to be brought from the well. When that happened, Dad used a sledge to bring the water up in churns to the house.

Elsie as a little girl

The farm had seven fields and two garths, which are smaller fields. We had a mare called Fanny who foaled every year, a few cows, some hens and sheep. The sheep used to go up on to Hardendale Nab where the local farmers had stints, which is so much land allotted to each farm. Besides keeping the animals, Dad grew potatoes, turnips and oats. Oh it was hard work at haytime. Dad used to mow in the mornings, then my mother and me would be out in the fields helping. I had to rake off the corners and turn the hay by hand. If the weather was bad all the hay had to be scattered again. We used a big rake – 'the old mare', that's what my dad called it. I had to trail the old mare backwards and forwards on that field, gathering all the 'rakings' as they were known. They don't bother to do that now.

There were only six little farms at Hardendale, and in winter it was very quiet. We did a bit of reading at night and some sewing but we usually went to bed fairly soon. Of course at that time of year it was pretty cold, with severe frosts. If you got caught in a blizzard coming home from school, you knew about it. When it was very bad we never went to school as we couldn't get over the stiles – the snow was so deep.

I'd started at Shap School when I was five and walked the one and a half miles from Hardendale when we moved there. I never liked going to school over the fields and my mother used to walk me part of the way. I hated the black cows in the fields – they were very inquisitive. I took my dinner with me, sandwiches and a little bottle of milk or tea. In wintertime the bottle of tea was put in front of the classroom fire but I had to remember to take the cork out or else it popped. Some of the children at school were from the Home, which had originally been the Workhouse. I think they had come from the Carlisle area but a lot stayed in Shap long after they left school, got jobs and settled down.

When the First World War was on we used to take eggs to school, put our name and address on them and they'd be sent to the soldiers. If you were lucky you got a letter from a soldier, which I did. We were also lucky at home during that time, as we had our own milk and butter. But the flour was horrible and made what we called black bread, which wasn't very nice at all. I suppose we got meat but it was rationed. I remember, one Christmas I was disgusted, as we just had sausages for dinner. I've never forgotten that. I thought it was terrible. Later, when we heard that the Armistice had been signed, I took the news home from Shap. We stuck a flag on top of the corn stack to celebrate.

It was pouring with rain on New Year's Day, 1915, when Mother and me travelled down to Gloucestershire. My brother was due to be born and we went to stay with my grandparents for three months. We travelled by horse and cart from the farm to Shap Station, where we caught the train down south. Mother's parents lived at a little place called Wilson's Folly, near Berkeley Castle where Grandad worked. When we came back home, all was spick and span. Dad had scrubbed out and even made butter and cooked bread while we'd been away.

Just after the war, my dad sold up and we lived in Shap for a year until we got a big farmhouse at Thrimby and Dad got a job working at Lowther's. There was such a big difference between Hardendale and Thrimby. At Hardendale in summer there were flowers different to anywhere else I've been. There was mealy primroses [*primula farinosa*], which are just like violets and eat insects. There was globe flowers,

dothering grass, cowslips, wild pansies and heather, of course. And birds
. . . there was any amount of grouse and pheasants but, apart from these
and crows and sparrows, you never saw any other birds. Thrimby was
different altogether. There was primroses, bluebells and Canterbury
bells. There was musk growing down by the river, star of Bethlehem and
violets you could find in the hedgerows. For birds, you got chaffinches,
bluetits, yellow hammers and wrens. And there was a corncrake in the
meadow opposite us.

The house that we moved to had been a big farmhouse with land to
it. Part of the land had gone to a farm and the other half had been taken
by Lowther Park. We still had a vegetable garden and orchard and of
course the toilet was outside. I remember sitting in there when a bit of
plaster came down from the ceiling. There was such a scuffle and a rat
dropped down and luckily it stunned itself. 'Golly, what am I going to do
with it?' I wondered. 'If I go for my cat, it'll probably have gone by the
time I get back.' I had my big shoes on, so I gave it one. Yes, I killed it. If
it had dropped down on my knee I would have had a fit, wouldn't I?

'Old Bob'

Just along the road from us was Old Bob Ebdale who used to work for Dargue's at Thornthwaite Hall. Bob lived with his sister who was a little old lady and didn't bother with anybody. As she was getting on in years, she had trouble with the buttonholes on the shirts she made for Bob, so I was paid a penny for each buttonhole that I did for her. Miss Ebdale had a lot of fruit bushes in her garden but it got so that she couldn't manage to make the jam with all this fruit. Anyway, she let me go and help her during my school holidays and I was amazed when I saw how she sealed the bottles. Once the jam was in the bottle, she put mutton fat on the top to seal it and then just a paper top over it. A relation of my father's, who was a widow, used to visit from Lancashire. When Miss Ebdale died, I asked this relation if she fancied a job as a housekeeper for Old Bob. Well by gum, they struck a bargain and it worked out fine. She kept house for him until he died.

Another family that I knew used to make crow pie. The men used to go out and shoot crows but it was only the breast of the bird that was used. Oh yes, crow pie was very nice and if the missus had any left she used to bring it to the house for us kids when we came home from school. That family had a big farm but all the land has been taken away now. A lot of it went when the motorway went through and our old house was pulled down.

I started at Little Strickland School which just had one room and two teachers. The boys and girls had a playground and a porch each, but when it was wet all the girls went to the boys' porch and we all danced while one boy played the mouth organ. They used to get a trip up every year and we went in Tom Simpson's wagon. It was a real day out and some of the parents came too. One year we went to Silloth and had a meal there and another time we went to Blackpool Carnival. It was crowded when we reached Blackpool, so we got on to a seat and sat there all day. But it was such a lovely day – there was dancing and all sorts. We'd never seen anything like it before. I joined the Lowther Girl Guides, which was smashing. We did all sorts of things and it really was the only bit of pleasure that I had because I didn't go anywhere and there was no one else to play with. We used to go camping and one year we went to Seascale.

At Christmas all the local children were invited to Lowther Castle for a Christmas party. Oh, it was beautiful. We were in the picture gallery and there was a huge tree with a fairy doll on top. This was the first Christmas tree I'd really seen and it was lovely. In the gallery there was pictures, of course, and they were as big as the walls. But the pictures weren't very pretty – just of horses and hunting, that sort of thing. The fireside was huge, with great lumps of coal on the fire and a basket of logs by the side. All the logs were shaved smooth so that there was no spiels [splinters] on them. When Lord Lowther came into the room he had a little horse and cart – not a real one, just a toy, but it was full of sweets for everyone. All the children got a present and then we would go and have our tea in the servants' quarters. You should have seen the toilets there, they were marvellous. I could have stopped there all day.

At Christmas all the village got a blanket and a joint of beef each from Lord Lowther. When the deer was being culled everybody got a bit of venison, so we didn't do too bad off him really. When the strike of 1926 was on, we could go to Lowther Park and get branches that had blown down, as we couldn't get any coal. On 12th August ('The Glorious Twelfth') we used to watch people going from Lowther up on to the moors for the grouse shooting. First of all the ponies would go past our house, then the big van with all the food, and finally the big canary yellow cars.

Royalty often came to stay at Lowther. I remember seeing the Prince of Wales arrive and also Princess Mary and Lord Lascelles. We used to call him Lord Lace Holes. Once, when Princess Mary was at the castle, the guides were to be inspected by her on the terrace. However that morning it snowed, so we were taken into the picture gallery and the only thing I can remember about Princess Mary is her thin legs. Lowther Castle was lovely and the gardens were gorgeous. It used to be a shilling to go into the grounds. There was rose gardens, a Japanese garden and some sunken gardens.

I didn't leave school, I just carried on. My idea was to be either a confectioner or a dressmaker but the headmistress suggested teaching. My parents didn't object so that was it – I sat an entrance exam and was accepted. It was decided to move me to Lowther Endowed School at Hackthorpe as a trainee teacher. There was a few of us training and we had to do a correspondence course. This was sent to us every week and consisted of English, history, geography and maths.

The course was more or less the same subjects that we did in class. Once a week we had to teach and do a criticism lesson. You had to prepare the lesson, write down what you were going to do and what you expected the children to learn from it. We were paid twenty-eight shillings a month, which we thought was great. Of the other students, one was from Crosby Ravensworth and two from Shap. Those that had to travel to school on their bikes were given a travel allowance of fifteen bob a year.

When students were eighteen they went to Kendal for a week to take the 'matric' exams. Three or four of us went together and lodged at Highgate and went to the technical college each day for our exams.

When you passed the 'matric', the Education Office sent a list of vacancies which you could apply for. I applied for Patterdale, Asby and Milburn, which were all in Westmorland, and was given Greenholme. I started at the school on 1st June, which was a Friday, and thought, 'Oh aye, my dad doesn't believe in starting a job on a Friday. I won't be here long.' But I was. I was at Greenholme for twelve years.

Greenholme is a hamlet, along from Orton. A river ran through the hamlet, which consisted of the school, schoolhouse, about five cottages and a farm. Old Mrs Johnstone kept the only shop and sold little bits of stuff that folk would run out of. The outlying farms reached up to Bretherdale and children from there came to our school. The school had two rooms – the smaller was mine and the larger one was Miss Hallam's. We had about fifty pupils and I taught the younger ones, from five up to eight years old. I hadn't been at the school very long when Miss Hallam's mother died and I had to run the school all on my own for a while. Some of the lads there were fourteen and ready for leaving school but, young as I was, they were no bother whatsoever.

Playtime at Greenholme School in the 1920s (Elsie is seated, centre)

For teaching, I'd take the little ones while I gave the others something else to do and then move on to the bigger ones. We had tables and so many spellings every week, which I think is a good way to learn. I always had a chart with the kiddies' names on it for their spellings. Then at the end of term we counted up who had the most correct. I would give a little prize to the winners – maybe a bar of chocolate or a tiny book.

They were all good little kiddies. I remember once, three kiddies from the same family started together. They were seven, six and five years old and came together because they were from away up on the fell. Another time I had three children from different families start at the same time who couldn't speak properly. I had to take all three and teach them how to speak and I managed it, though I'd never been taught anything like that. I got them to sound their words and the letters, that sort of thing. You see, some children if they have older brothers and sisters won't be bothered to talk because the older ones know what they want.

In wintertime teachers were asked here, there and everywhere, especially at Christmas. We'd be invited to someone's home for a meal or to play cards – that's what they used to do in country districts. Then we had concerts and plays. Everybody joined in, all the kiddies and people from round about. We'd have a sketch with the adults and the farm men would come and sing. One play that we did, all the men taking part needed to wear wigs with curls on them. The lady who made the costumes went round all the cows and cut the curls from their tails for these wigs. We did laugh but the curls looked really good when she had finished with them.

My wage when I started teaching was £11 a month. At first I travelled daily from home by bus to Orton, where I found somewhere to leave my bike, and then rode to Greenholme. But when the buses were knocked off, I lodged at Highscales Farm near the school and paid fifteen bob a week. At weekends I went home on Friday and came back on Monday morning.

A correspondent from the Education Authority used to come and visit the school once a month. He'd bring our wages and look down the register to see if there was anything we needed. As our correspondent, Mr Wharton, was getting on in years, eventually I used to call at his house for our wages and let him know if we needed anything. The Education Authority also employed inspectors to come round the schools and look at the work we were doing. They just looked at the work or maybe suggested improvements.

When the Second World War started, there was quite a few evacuees from the Newcastle area. Being from big towns, some of them didn't know what potatoes were. It had been all chips. These kiddies would get their eyes opened, with the cattle, sheep and all the countryside, and some of them didn't care for it. They were used to towns and houses, so I think they felt a bit lost. But I remember two of them, Donald and his brother Dick. Do you know, they came back to this area recently for a visit and they managed to trace me. After fifty years!

My husband was a blacksmith at Orton. I met him when I was waiting for the bus and he came and talked to me. Maybe a month later there was some sports and then a dance at Little Strickland and George came. At this dance there was George and another lad that I rather liked, so I said to myself, 'Aye well, the one that asks me to go for my supper, that'll be the one.' Well, it was George, so that's how it happened. He'd come to the dance on a motorbike and brought another chap with him. So when he took me home, there was me sitting between these two lads on a motorbike.

In those days you had to leave teaching when you married and it was another ten years before I could teach again. My wedding wasn't much at all because it was wartime. We had the reception at my home and there was only George's parents and mine there. It wasn't a big do and my wedding cake had no icing on it because there was no sugar to be had. It was a lovely cake though, with a big ribbon round it, that had been made at the Co-op at Penrith.

George and I went to live at a little cottage at Orton which had one room and a pantry downstairs and two bedrooms upstairs. Outside was the toilet (but it was a flush one) and a little wash-house. At one time Orton had been a very busy and important village because it sported a market. The Market Hall still exists and is used for village functions. Up to the 1930s, a Tup Fair was held every October when the farmers brought all their tups to sell and pens were erected all over the village. At night a dance was held in the Market Hall. A great do that was, with all the girls dressed up in their finery. The boys always had their 'bird seed' [drink] to give them courage, so it all went with a swing.

Years before, my husband's grandfather farmed at Burtree near Asby and often visited Orton, riding a faithful old horse. Like most men at that time, he indulged in alcohol. He had to be helped on to the horse's back and it took him home from Orton.

My husband was working for Croft's, the agricultural engineers at Kendal, by this time. He was away all week, putting milk machines in on the farms, so I only saw him at weekends. George travelled all over Cumberland and Westmorland and down to Barrow. As he had to stay at the farms he was working at, the farmers had to supply him with food. All sorts of places he got to, funny ones and some not very pleasant but usually the people were very good to him. With having George's ration book, we didn't do so bad.

We'd only been at Orton for three years when my father-in-law died. That left George's mother, sister and her two sons alone on their farm. George said to me, 'If I can get a big house in Kendal, what about us all living together?' I said 'No' at the time but he didn't take any notice and went ahead. What a state the house was in! It was a good house but there'd been an old lady living in it who had lots of cats. She hadn't been able to do much and it stank, it really did. When my sister-in-law and I came to clean the house, we brought our sandwiches with us but couldn't eat them because of the smell. We had to take the food to the top of the house to eat it and it was a three-storey house.

All living together worked out well. We made it work – you had to in those days. George's family lived with us until they got another house and we had a couple of years on our own. Then my father died and my mother came to us for eighteen years, until she died at ninety-three years of age.

My first son was born during the war when we were still at Orton. In those days you weren't really given much help or advice. I don't think I even went to the doctor's to have it confirmed that I was expecting. You just carried on as normal, as best you could. When the baby was due to be born the district nurse and doctor came but the nurse couldn't stay long. It was snowing like mad and, as she lived with her old mother who was ninety, she had to get herself back home. Oh it did snow, it was awful. I don't know how my husband managed to get home that weekend. At that time there was a maternity hospital at Kendal but I couldn't have got there even if I'd wanted to, with all the snow. My second son was born at the end of the war and I did go into hospital to have him. Unfortunately the heating system broke down while I was there and, being October, it was starvation [freezing].

When I started teaching again I did supply work so I was here, there and everywhere. It was a bit of all right was supply teaching, and I was at most of the schools in Kendal. Eventually I was taken on permanently at Castle Street School, which was a mixed primary and a lovely school. It was such a friendly place, it really was. We used to have coffee mornings and rummage sales which were fun. At Christmastime the older kids were told to go and make up a play. Then they would perform it on the stage before we had our holiday. We had many a laugh as they used to get up to all sorts of things, but they were really good you know.

At Castle Street I had up to forty-eight pupils in a class but now you can't have more than thirty. So Castle Park School was built and we moved there where I stayed until I retired. I really enjoyed teaching,

Staff at Castle Park School (Elsie is in the front row, second from the left)

they were all grand kids that I had and the other teachers were very good.

Looking back, life was much more peaceful, and the people were really more friendly and helpful. And the countryside was far more beautiful because there was more vegetation and flowers. There's been a lot of changes – though at least we don't have to blacklead grates now. I had a good upbringing. My clothes were decent, even if I only got one frock a year. We weren't well off but we were well cared for and weren't short of anything really.

'It was like a floating population in our house'

ANNIE DAWSON (b. 1914)
Keswick

My mother was only thirteen in 1902 when she left Keswick to go and work in London. Some relations found her a job as a court dressmaker but she got fed up with this, saying it was too tedious. Mother then went into service and worked in one of those big houses in Eaton Square for a Member of Parliament. Later she returned to Keswick and married my father who was a groomsman for Mr and Mrs Slack of Derwent Hill.

I was born in January 1914, in a little house behind the Main Street of Braithwaite. It's called Main Street now but I've always known it as Duck Street. I can't remember living there because we moved to Portinscale, and when the Great War started my father joined up straight away.

During the Great War my mother and I seemed to commute between Keswick and Buxton in Derbyshire, where her mother owned a large house and took in visitors. Grandma's main home was in Keswick and I think some relation had left her this property. When we were at Buxton my mother would cook, her sister did the housework and Grandma looked after me and my cousin. However Grandma decided to visit her eldest daughter, Agnes, who was married and had a lot of children. Aunt Agnes lived in Canada and Grandma had a horrific journey because there was all these U-boats and Lord knows what following the ship. So, once Grandma got to Canada, she couldn't get back until the end of the war.

Dad was lucky, as he came out of the war without a scratch. My mother used to say that when he came home on leave he was absolutely filthy with lice. When the Great War finished there seemed to be all sorts of festivities and parades but no job for my father. We moved to Manchester for a short time, then came back and lived at Braithwaite, before moving to Swinside, which is up in Newlands village. By this time I had a brother, who was born in 1919.

When we lived at Swinside I had to walk to Braithwaite School,

31

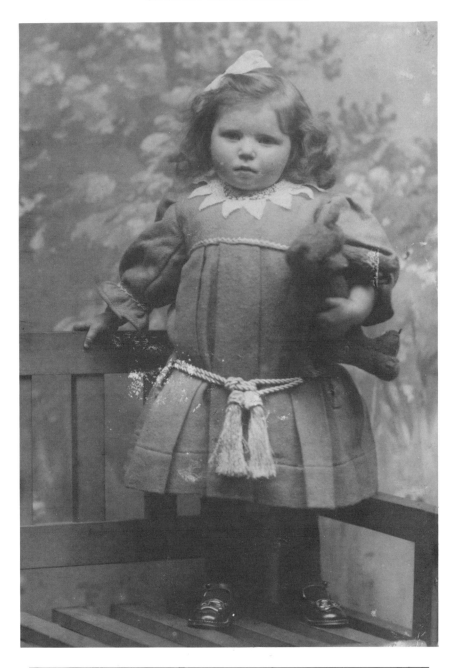

Above: Annie in a dress made by her mother, a court dressmaker Right:
Annie's cousin, Jonty Robinson, collecting for charity with his pet hen during
the 1914–18 war, on the steps of what is now the Midland Bank, Keswick

which was about two and a half miles away. I'm left-handed but when I started school it was decided that I had to learn to write with my right hand. At nights I had to take a copy book home and practise my writing. But it did seem odd, using this right hand. When a new headmaster came he didn't mind that I was left-handed but I used to get into trouble with the sewing teacher and had to try and use my other hand again. So I would turn the sewing upside down and sew with my left hand. Then it looked as if I'd used my right hand.

A couple of years later Dad got his job back with the Slacks. They needed a chauffeur and Dad could drive, so we moved back to Portinscale and lived in a cottage on the Derwent Hill estate. The cottage next door also belonged to the estate and an old lady called Mrs Bentley lived there, who was one of the gardeners. We never knew where Dad was because the Slacks toured all over the place – Scotland or down to the south of England. One winter they spent in the south of France and Dad was with them.

My mother also helped in the kitchens for the old Lord and Lady Rochdale when they had pheasant shoots. She was thrilled to bits because, with being in service before, she knew all the 'ins and outs'. You see, years ago there were jobs like this, as there was a lot of gentry. I think most of them were industrialists who built big houses in the district. A lot of the staff were girls from the mining villages of West Cumberland where there was no work for them. So they came to the Keswick area and worked in the shops, hotels or big houses, and they were hard workers. Many of them married local men and stayed. One of my grandmothers came from Maryport to find work, then married my grandfather.

After the Great War there was a recession, just like there is now, and we used to have tramps come to our house and beg for a cup of tea. My mother was very, very kind and always used to give them a sandwich or even put a fried egg in for them. Some of the men were tramps but others were just wandering about the countryside looking for work. They really were desperate and it was sad.

Circuses used to travel past our house on the Cockermouth to Keswick road. If we knew there was a circus my brother and me would get up early in the morning to watch them go by. Of course there was no motor transport then – it was all horse-drawn wagons. Once we were watching for the horses coming and saw the funniest thing. A man was leading a camel that had a lantern round its neck and an elephant with some sort of leather shoes on its feet. It was most peculiar. As it was about six o'clock in the morning, they would have walked all night from Cockermouth. We went to greet the man and my mother said to him, 'Oh, you'll have to have a cup of tea.' So, while the man was having his cup of tea, this elephant was putting its trunk over the garden gate looking for something to eat.

Every year we had a May Day, which was a lovely day for the kids. It was started by Canon Rawnsley in the last century and it was connected with the Band of Hope. You never hear of the Band of Hope these days, do you? Keswick had four 'Hope' bands. There was Crosthwaite, St John's, Congregational and Southey Street Methodist. Then there was the four county ones: Braithwaite, Portinscale, Applethwaite and I think Brigham. A singing competition was held in the morning and in the afternoon there'd be a parade round Keswick. A May Queen used to ride on a pony in the parade and she'd wear a crown and carry a staff of lilies. She had sixteen attendants who walked beside her, dressed in white and carrying baskets of flowers. Each year the May Queen was chosen from one of the districts, so each section had their turn. After the parade we would go into the park and there'd be sports before we went for tea. At night there was a concert in the Pavilion and the May Queen would be crowned by the previous year's Queen. It was a good day out but kids wouldn't bother now. It's too old-fashioned, isn't it?

People had coughs and colds but I don't think there was that much illness. The only time people were really ill was when they got scarlet fever and had to go to the fever hospital. This was like a cottage hospital up on Whinlatter Pass and patients had to stay there for six weeks. There was a sanatorium at Threlkeld for TB but not many locals seemed to go there – it was mostly people from the mining areas of West Cumberland.

I wasn't clever enough to win a scholarship and go to the Grammar School. You see, years ago when you reached fourteen you never stopped on at school unless you went to the Grammar and then you went on until you were sixteen. Your parents looked for a job for you – you had no choice in the matter really. My mother thought, 'Well, she's not going into service', and she heard there was some jobs going at Abrahams, the photographers. She went to see Mr Ashley Abraham, he took a few particulars, and about Eastertime in 1928 I started as an apprentice printer.

Abrahams shop was on Borrowdale Road at Keswick and the workshops were in some buildings across the road. My first day at work was cold, damp and wet – that was the darkroom. In wintry weather it would be starvation [freezing]. Later on I used to go and do enlarging up in the tower above the main shop and oh, it was cold. We used acetic acid and it used to freeze solid in the bottles. We had to come downstairs to warm them up in front of a stove.

For work we all wore black overalls and looked like black widows. There were three or four apprentices, all girls, and we were paid four shillings and sixpence a week. It went up each year and by the time we finished our five-year apprenticeship the wage was ten shillings. When we came out of our time, the wage went right up to one pound and five shillings. Oh, we thought we were millionaires.

I biked to work from Portinscale and left the bike at my grandma's where I went to eat my lunch and tea. We had an hour off for both meals but we did put in some long hours. In winter I started work at half-past eight in the morning and finished at half-six at night. Come summer, I finished at seven o'clock and at half-seven when it was Whitsun. At Convention time I worked a twelve-hour day. And we had no half-day off – only on a Wednesday we finished at four p.m.

We were trained in how to print, enlarge and develop by others who had served their time. The person who taught me a lot was married and she'd come back to help out. But when most of the apprentices got more used to doing their jobs, like everywhere else they were paid off. Then the Abrahams would get another batch of apprentices and start again, but I was lucky enough to be kept on. I enjoyed the work and I suppose I was good at it.

Mr Ashley and Mr George, the two famous climbing, Abraham brothers, ran the business. They were both all right. Mr George was quieter than Mr Ashley who could snap your head off. Both were very, very particular about what was turned out. You had to show a proof if you were doing a batch of prints, to see if it was right. They wouldn't turn out any shoddy stuff at all. Just a couple of people worked in the shop but hundreds and thousands of black and white postcards were sold. Mr Ashley had a lot of agents and in the springtime they'd go touring around to shops and places that sold the cards.

The Abrahams didn't do much portraiture, mostly landscapes. They went climbing all over the place – to Scotland, Wales, the Alps and the Dolomites. The photos they took were all on eight by six inch plates, not like it is now on thirty-five millimetre film and blown up. Usually it was professional people, such as businessmen, who went climbing and there wasn't the handsome equipment like there is today.

I had my photograph taken a few times by the Abrahams. They had a contract with a slate quarry up at Honister for advertising photos and I was asked, 'Do you have a flat hat?' Well, we all wore hats in those days, so I had my photo taken wearing my hat and best two-piece. I was supposed to be a customer looking at the slate on houses. Then later, just before the war, the Geographical Society who had a monthly magazine got in touch with the Abrahams about taking colour photos of the Lake District. For quite a few weeks I went around in a Daimler with them,

Mr Abraham with Annie in her flat hat, pretending to be a customer

while they were taking photos. There was a photo taken of me in a nice green dress and hat, stepping into this Daimler outside Rydal Church.

The Co-op used to cover both sides of St John's Street, it was that big. Once a year they had a big party and the Abrahams took the photos of it. It was a big fancy dress party and whist drive, which was a great affair. They used to have lovely prizes, like suites of furniture. Then when the Convention was taking place photos would be taken of people coming out of the tent at Helvellyn Street. When it was the Diamond Jubilee of the Convention the organisers wanted a super photograph with as many people on it as possible. The big Convention tent held 5,000 people so a big gantry was rigged up at a field called Brow Ridding. A twelve by ten inch camera was used and all those people were on this photograph. We did every plate by hand, so I can tell you it was a hectic Convention. But I enjoyed my life at Abrahams, I really did.

The Keswick Convention was started over 100 years ago in a tent in the grounds of St John's Church. It was for all Protestant religions, and a lot of missionaries came to speak about their experiences abroad. I think in those days the Convention only lasted ten days but now it's held in the second and third weeks of July. The first service used to be held at seven o'clock in the morning. Then people would have their breakfast before returning to later meetings.

On Wednesday it was the big meeting for the missionaries in one of the big tents. There used to be two big tents but the one on Eskin Street has gone now and the meetings are all held in a big complex down Skiddaw Street. When the Convention was on, people used to camp all over the place in different fields and it used to be awful when the weather was bad. The town is still as busy for the Convention, and at the church I attend we sell soup, pies, sausage rolls – you name it, we make it. There's always a queue and if it's fine we put tables and chairs outside. It's just like a tea party but it's hard work I can tell you.

I lived at Portinscale from 1924 until 1934, when Mr Slack died and his whole estate was wound up. As we were living in a tied house, Mum and Dad had to find a place in Keswick. We landed up at 27 Church Street and Dad got a job as a postman. My mother used to do dinner, bed and breakfast. In those days people used to get ready for the Easter trade early in the year and carry on until the end of September. After that everybody closed down. It was hard work and I vowed and declared that I'd never have a guesthouse.

At the beginning of 1939 there was a recruitment drive for the Territorial Army and my future husband and his pals decided to join up in the spring. They had a summer camp at the end of August and the war started on 3rd September. That was it – my husband was in the Army

37

from day one. The Government must have known there was going to be a bust-up of some sort to have had the recruitment drives.

My goodness, the difference the war made to Keswick. When it first started we were absolutely inundated with Jewish people. Most of them came up from London and were petrified, as they thought Hitler was going to invade London there and then. With having a guesthouse, my mother had some Turkish Jews staying. They had factories which made underwear in the East End of London, so I got myself fixed up with underwear for the duration of the war.

After a while, when things quietened down, all these people just drifted away and after them came the evacuees. Keswick was packed out with evacuees during the war. There was Roedean School from Brighton, which took over the Keswick Hotel and the Millfield Hotel. The boys from the High School at Newcastle were sent to Penrith and the girls came to Keswick. They wore brown uniforms and for some reason we called them 'The Brown Bombers'. The Driving and Maintenance School took over the Derwentwater Hotel and nearly all the garages. It was nothing to see a bren gun carrier stuck up on Latrigg or Walla Cragg. A college from Liverpool was in the Queen's Hotel and the Tower Hotel at Portinscale. We were absolutely swamped with evacuees.

Every now and again commandos would come and train locally, so we used to get soldiers billeted with us. To tell you the truth, it was like a floating population in our house. You never knew who was in and who wasn't. The forces personnel, especially, seemed to move about. They used to come for a week or two's training and they'd be off and we'd get another lot.

My future in-laws had two little girls staying from Birmingham and I seemed to spend half my time looking after them. You see, my husband's parents didn't have time to look after the children as they were the caretakers of St John's School and the library. Schooling was done in shifts, with some pupils attending in the morning and others in the afternoon, as they couldn't accommodate them all at the same time.

The Abrahams did quite a lot of trade, as they got the contract with the Driving and Maintenance School to take the photographs of the new batches of soldiers. Being the only one left to do any printing and look after the shop, I wasn't called up. The best thing was that we had to close early because of all the big windows on the premises. They would never have been able to black them out. The business was very antiquated and after the war, when Mr Ashley's son took over, he modernised the place.

I was married in December 1941. Because of the war, the wedding was an ordinary affair and I wore a plain blue dress and hat. The reception was at my mother's house, with about twenty guests. My mother-in-law made a three-tiered wedding cake, and where she got the ingredients from I don't know. We just had a little reception and stayed at Blackpool with some relations for three days because my husband had to go back to his unit again.

My eldest son was born at my mother's house but the next two children were born at a private nursing home. I think a maternity unit had started up in Penrith after the war but I wouldn't go to a hospital. There was a little private nursing home at Penrith, so I went there. It was nice. It was like a holiday really because I was looked after and had my own bedroom. Every patient had their own tray with a little china teapot on, it was lovely. The nurse wouldn't let anyone get up for the first week after the birth and we stayed at the home for two weeks. It wasn't like it is now. Women seem as though they're on a conveyor belt now, don't they?

When I got married my husband belonged to Crosthwaite Church and was a handbell ringer for them. I got roped in and only retired about five years ago. There was about ten of us and we went all over the county playing the handbells. We especially enjoyed going to the Women's Institutes because they always put on a good feed. When Russell Harty was going around the countryside doing some programmes we went on one of the lake steamers at Windermere and gave a demonstration for him.

My husband and myself loved walking on the fells and taught our sons to enjoy it too. If we had a day off through the week – but usually on a Sunday – we'd be out and about. After our boys had come out of Sunday School we'd either go off for a picnic on the fells or borrow a cousin's boat and row across the lake to the island. Oh, we did enjoy it. I'd take sausages with us, a jelly in a milk carton and a fruit pasty. My sons still enjoy going on the fells. One of them thinks nothing about running up and down Grizedale Pike. I wouldn't have liked to live anywhere else – this is my home. There isn't anywhere else like Keswick, with the lake and mountains.

Years ago there was a man called Tom Wilson who was a great Keswickian and thought a lot about the town. He got together an organisation and a magazine, which was called P.U.P.s (Pushing Young People). Mr Wilson used to get up all sorts of whist drives, dances and carnivals. He thought everybody should stick to Keswick and his magazine was all about the district. It was good and there was some really funny things in it, as well as local history.

I still have the first two magazines from 1932 and the article about old Keswick. You see, in this town there aren't many of the old yards left and there was such a lot of places that's all gone now. Chitty Puss Lane, that

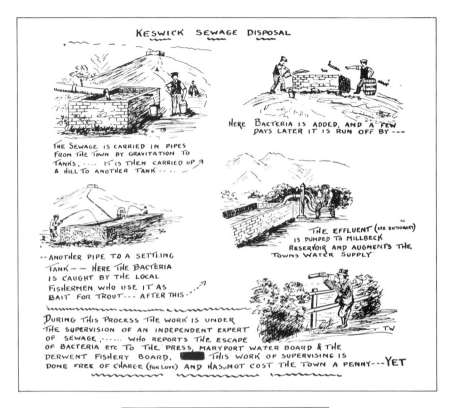

Extract from the P.U.P.'s Annual, 1932

really was Pear Tree Lane, that's gone. Somerbirks Brow is now the main street. Shu-le-le-Crow is the hill coming into Keswick where the war memorial is. Shambles Yard, I think that's the Packhorse Court now. There's the Plosh, that's some little cottages along Borrowdale Road. Dixon's Gates is a little alleyway that leads from the Royal Oak onto Lake Road. We always used to call it Paraffin Alley because that's what it smelt of. Frying Pan Square, that's on top of Derwent Street but it's St John's something or other now. Ladies Dub was a little bit of the River Greta in Fitz Park. Now it's all built up but we used to go and play in Ladies Dub because it was all nice and sandy.

Why the railway station was shut down I just don't know. It was a lovely little station. We haven't got the Pavilion any more and the Abrahams business sold out in 1967, a year after their hundredth anniversary. I'm about the only one left that used to work there. Now when I go out into all these cafés and restaurants, what am I confronted with? All Abrahams photos and prints on their walls.

FOUR

'I'm the oldest woman left from Allonby'

NORAH EDGAR (b. 1906)
Allonby

I was an only child born in 1906, and as my dad died when I was about three I really don't remember much about him. My mother and I lived with my uncle, aunt and three cousins at Bridge House, Allonby. This was a cottage and a house combined – Mother and I were in the cottage and the others in the house. It was really the Mill House, and both the house and the mill had been in our family since 1720.

My mother and aunt worked together at home and did their cooking on a black range, with an oven by the side and a boiler that supplied the hot water. For lighting, we had candles and little Aladdin lamps which were a nuisance and smelled. If you touched the middle part of the lamp it spoilt and you had to buy another one, which worked out expensive. There was no bathroom but we did have a great big bath and we would put it in front of the fire, locking the doors before getting in. There had been a pump outside that supplied water but that was before my time.

In those days women had different days for doing their work. Washing day was Wednesday and bedroom day was Thursday and so on. But my mother was never well and, as Auntie had her children fast, they had a woman in to wash and clean. I remember, when the washing was done it was carried across onto the shore and stones put on to hold it down while it dried. That is going back but – sheets, pillowcases or whatever – nobody touched them and they got nice and white.

As I was brought up with my boy cousins, we all played together and I was like a boy myself. We played together near the mill, which was just across the bridge from where we lived. Inside the mill it was dark and we would sit on the kiln to play where it was nice and warm. Unless my uncle was watching us, we hadn't to go near the mill wheel. It was too dangerous.

The local farmers brought their cereal to the mill, where it was ground, bagged and put into the warehouse until they came with their carts to carry it away. I know my uncle was kept busy all year with the mill, as farmers only brought their cereal to be ground when they needed it.

Opposite the house was the wash-house, potato house and the place where the pig, horse and three cows were kept. As children, we never saw the pig being killed. People used everything from a pig and up on our ceiling we had hooks which we used to put sides of bacon on. The bacon was wrapped up and used all winter. In fact it was used all the time until it was finished. Neighbours who killed their pig would give us some part they had saved and we gave them whatever we could.

I never learnt how to milk cows but I used to go into the byre, and in those days candles were used for light until Candlemas. At Candlemas it was said to be light enough not to use a candle and you could see to do the milking. Our cows were in the byre all winter, and when they were let out in spring they used to go absolutely mad. These cows would gallop up and down the bridge and we couldn't help but laugh to see them. My uncle had a field about a mile down the school lane and I used to take the cows there in the morning and bring them back at night. Unfortunately I didn't have time to do this when I was older, with having so much homework.

Auntie had a big dairy where the cream was skimmed off the top of the milk and some of it was used to make butter. It was Auntie's job to sell this cream and butter from the house, which people collected in cans. Allonby people never went to Maryport Market to sell their butter, as there was plenty of locals who would buy it. When we did go to Maryport we travelled in a digby which was a little open trap with sides to it, oval-shaped and driven by pony.

At Christmas I would get an apple and an orange and little presents like a pair of stockings. One year, I remember I got a pair of gloves and in one glove there was a halfpenny in each finger. We always had a goose at Christmas and a lot of relations came and celebrated. However in 1912 some relations, the Brays from Allonby, emigrated to Canada and they had an awful time at first. When they reached Nova Scotia one of their sons got an ear infection and had to stay in hospital and that took most of their money.

The rest of our relations went out to Canada later that year and we thought about going, but they said Mother wouldn't stand the climate as she was too delicate. So the only family left was the seven of us at Bridge House. Some of these relations came back for a holiday when I was older and one cousin with bobbed hair said, 'I've learned to Charleston on the boat.' Away she went with her legs and I was amazed – I'd never seen anything like that before. People emigrated in those days because they had the chance to go and there wasn't the work here.

Allonby School, 1911 (Norah is in the front row, third from the right

I was four and a half when I started at Allonby School, which was a good little school with two rooms, one for the infants and one for the older kiddies. The headmaster was Mr Cushing and his wife also taught, which was unusual as married women weren't allowed to teach in those days. Then there was Miss Bott and Miss Jefferson, who was from Hayton. I went home at dinnertime as I didn't live so far away, but the ones who stayed at school had little tea cans which were put on the classroom stove to keep warm. During the First World War we had three Belgian evacuees at school. They wore black smocks, not like our clothes, and we sort of made fun of them at first but we got used to these kiddies and accepted them as ordinary people. I remember that Mr Cushing got these evacuees to teach us all to sing the French national anthem. About this time, there was some disabled soldiers at Allonby living in a big house with a verandah, which must have been a convalescent home.

My youngest cousin, who emigrated to Canada when he was fourteen, joined up and came back to England as a soldier during the First World War. He came to see us three times and I can still see him waving to us, the last time he left. We never saw him again, he was killed in action in April 1918. After the war finished we used to celebrate War Day at school. It was just a cup of tea and sandwiches affair that parents attended but it didn't last many years.

We had a Sports Day at Allonby from when I was tiny until I was grown up. It was on the Silloth side of the village, on the Green, and visitors won most of the prizes. I never won anything, I couldn't run fast enough. Everybody went to the Sports. It was a big occasion, a full day with a marquee where a dance was held at night. That was the one day of the year when a man with a horse and cart came from Maryport to sell fish and chips. It was the only time we could buy chips and the man would do a good trade.

In Allonby, the locals did an awful lot of taking in visitors and we used to let our house in summer to a doctor from Glasgow. People would let their houses and move into a smaller cottage, as visitors brought their own staff to do the work. The money that local people made from the visitors would keep them all winter. Allonby was a popular place. People came from all over the country and played on the sands and swam. As kiddies, we had no swimming lessons but we were in the water every day. We learnt to swim by waiting until the tide was coming in, so we would be carried ashore with it.

The village was just about the same size as it is now. There was Miss Strong who sold sweets and vegetables in a shop in the Square. I was frightened of her as she was one of those sort that shouted at you. Costin's shop was very similar but for some reason we got all our groceries from Miss Strong. Then Mrs Richardson ran a sweetshop, while her husband worked as a painter and decorator.

The cake shop in the village was run by the Harrisons. There was Mr Harrison and his three sisters, all of them unmarried. One sister did the baking, one cleaned and the other one served in the shop. They also employed a girl who went round the village with a basket, selling cakes, and at Eastertime she sold hot cross buns. On that day we never had any breakfast until we had a bun, which wouldn't cost more than a penny. Oh, the toffee that Harrisons made was great. Allonby Toffee it was called. Now that's something Allonby was famous for – its toffee. It was made in great big blocks, and when you went into the shop they cut off bits with nippers and weighed it for you. Do you know, they didn't leave the recipe. The Harrisons died one after the other and the recipe died with them.

Before my time there had been seven pubs in Allonby but when I was little there was just the Globe, the Ship and the Grapes. I had one relation who had been educated and went to London where he got into bad company and had to come back. He married and had a big family but when he got drunk at the pub he used to come home and throw things out of the bedroom window for people to take away. Oh, he was terrible, terrible, but he grew better as he got older. I adored him and used to sit on his knee, thinking he was grand.

I'll tell you what there was . . . That awful building near the bridge that's all boarded up, it used to be the Reading Room. You see, nobody in Allonby got daily papers. These were delivered to the Reading Room. That's where all the men used to go to read the papers and play billiards.

There was naughtiness in those days. Some of the village boys used to throw people's barrows in the mill dam and things like that. They also used to go round to people's windows and play tricks, which I did as well – fasten a button on to the window by a thread and keep rattling it, or else knock and run away before the owners opened the door.

Once a year, a flock of geese were driven through the village by Irish drovers. They had come from Ireland to Silloth and were taking the geese on to Maryport. When they reached Allonby the geese were left on the village green and the drivers went into the Ship opposite for a drink and something to eat. Oh, there was a great lot of these geese to make it worth their while and all the kiddies used to crowd round the green to watch them eating grass or resting. Poor things, driven all the way from Silloth to Maryport and coming from Ireland.

I didn't know much about the village policeman until I was about seven or eight and a woman drowned. We were playing down on the sands and this boy said, 'Oh, there's a woman floating.' We all went to look and could see this woman with long black hair, a white blouse and a black skirt floating on the waves. We ran for Mr Sessford, the policeman, who went into the water and dragged her by the skirt out of the water and put her body into the hearse. I never slept that night with thinking about that woman. She was from Flimby.

I had to go to church and Sunday School every Sunday. We used to go on Sunday School trips in a wagonette and I first went when I was four and a half. I know when we arrived at Bassenthwaite I didn't dare go anywhere and just played around the wagonette because I was so nervous. We often had a wet day for these outings and when that happened we went into a shop at Bassenthwaite to buy nougat.

The fishing boats in the village were mostly before my time, and when I was young they were being broken up by a Mr Dixon as fishing was dying out. I know a family called Twentyman went fishing. They were the last ones and they used to come round every night selling codlings [young cod] on a string which we bought for our supper. The Twentymans came to Allonby many, many years ago and their boats were kept on the banks. As kiddies we used to go and watch them mending their nets but it was the grandfather who'd really been the fisherman. A long time ago one of my relations, who wasn't married and must have been fairly rich, died at Allonby and left my grandfather a boat called the *Mary Rose*. I've still got that will.

Workington Technical School, 1912, from Vulcan Park

At twelve years old we sat a test at school which five of us, three girls and two boys, passed. This was the test to go to the Technical School at Workington. The girls had to wear navy blue uniforms and white blouses and the boys had to wear white shirts. The five of us biked to Bullgill Station every day and travelled from there by train to Workington. Our bicycles were left at a house at Bullgill, which cost us a penny each a week. When I was at the Technical School I won a prize for grammar and it had all been what Mr Cushing had taught us at Allonby. So he was good, was Mr Cushing. But I know I got a lot of homework, a terrible lot of homework, and spent most of my time doing it.

I was never very good at hockey at school. You see, in winter when we were playing hockey we had to catch an earlier train home. The teacher often forgot what time it was and I would miss that train. I used to be terrified cycling on my own, down from Bullgill to Allonby, when it was dark.

At sixteen years of age we studied for the matriculation examination which consisted of seven subjects. I got credits for all seven subjects, so I did rather well. Then another girl, two boys and myself attended Aspatria School for tuition to be trainee teachers. We travelled from home every day, Monday to Thursday, and on Friday we went back to school at Workington. Aspatria was a very big village in those days and the Council School was old-fashioned and had standards, as the classes were called. It was a big school with seven classes, which was why we were sent there. Each trainee teacher sat in a classroom taking notes and learned how to teach by listening. We didn't teach, just watched every standard being taught and learnt all that we could. I remember every Thursday night when I was cycling home I stayed for tea at an old-fashioned village pub at West Newton. It was run by a lady who I called Auntie Annie as she was a distant relation. She was an old, unmarried lady who ran the pub on her own.

I left school when I was eighteen as Mother was very ill and needed looking after. Mr Cushing at Allonby School was very, very good to me and asked me to teach at his school. Then I was near home and Mother. I'd had no training but, as we were all teaching in one big classroom, he kept an eye on me. He showed me what to do and I learnt from him and studying books at home, as there was no correspondence course.

On my first day at school I was put in charge of the middle children, seven- and eight-year-olds, and there was about twenty of them. I taught all the subjects, the three Rs, religious instruction, history, geography and nature study, and ran the netball team which did very well. One girl who played netball was nearly as tall as the hoop, so she was a real menace to the other teams.

Allonby School Netball Team, 1926
(Norah is standing behind the girls)

I remember being sent to a Maryport school to cover for sickness, and on the first day there I was handed the cane. I didn't know what to do with it and found that I had to cane all the latecomers. If any schools in the area were shortstaffed I was sent to cover and made my own way by bike. Though the schools were all different, the teaching was the same – it was always the three Rs.

My wage was very poor, about £2 a week, when I started teaching. I gave all this to my mother and my uncle gave us anything we needed, such as potatoes, eggs and milk. We had plenty of fun out of school. I went to whist drives, played tennis and went on bike rides. The tennis club was in a small field down by the school and was well supported before the war. It closed during the war, and when we opened up again the boys started a cricket club and that spoilt it as we hadn't so many members.

Allonby, 1930s

At Allonby we thought the Depression had passed us by. The village seemed to survive on its own and we thought we hadn't been hit. I know Dearham was hit by the Depression, as a friend was teaching there and they had soup for the children at school. Then we noticed our children at Allonby School were disappearing. The numbers went down from over eighty to about forty. You see, families were quietly leaving to go away and find work. With not having as many children at school, the middle teacher was cut out. So that was that – I had to leave.

I did temporary teaching at West Newton and Torpenhow, which was a long way to bike. At Torpenhow, I remember a little boy coming to school and saying, 'Guess what we've got at home?' It wasn't a new lamb or a foal and in great glee he said, 'We've got a new babby and me farther and me knew nowt about it.' One lovely tale I heard from Dearham School was when the teacher taught all the kiddies to ask individually at playtime, 'Please, may I go out and play?' The teacher would reply, 'Yes, out you go.' Once, when one little girl had been told she could go out and play, she turned to her friend and said, 'We can gar oot und laik noo.'

I didn't do relief teaching for very long before I went on a permanent basis to Gilcrux and I biked from home every day. Education hadn't changed, the other teachers kept an eye on me (with being a trainee), and we still taught all the subjects. Every year a man came from the Education Authority to examine all the work and books. He didn't tell us when he was coming, he just arrived. We also had the School Board man who made sure children went to school. If they didn't, he came after them and they had to go.

In 1931 the mill was sold, as the road had to be widened. Also, people had stopped coming to have their cereal ground, as a place at Silloth had started up which had a bigger stone. Mother and I still lived at the Bridge House. However, by the time the war started, Mother wasn't at all well. The doctor told me, 'You'll have to do something or you could come in one day and find her dead. But with great care, she could live longer.' You see, it was her heart and she was very, very thin, so Mother went into a private nursing home at Carlisle. I think I paid about thirty shillings towards her upkeep, as that was all I could afford.

A few years later my mother died, and a year after that my friend Dorothy also lost her mother, so we were both alone. In those days it was often expected that girls would look after their parents and sometimes they gave up quite a lot. I never married. My first boyfriend was out of work and had his mother to support. As I had my mother to look after, I packed him in. I couldn't stop working, as I needed to teach to support my mother. And also if I'd got married I would have had to give up my job. But with my mother and Dorothy's mother dying almost together, at least we were able to get out and about. We stayed in a big house on the front at Allonby for about a year, then moved into a nice little cottage.

There was rationing, of course, during the war but we had sufficient. We were always able to get a little bit extra butter or eggs and we managed. At the village schools an awful lot of the children's parents were exempt from the war, with being farmers. At the end of the war we had tea and celebrations in the village, then Dorothy and I biked to a dance at Aspatria.

I asked for a transfer when the war ended and I went to Holme St Cuthbert's School which was about a mile inland from Mowbray. The children who attended the school came from around the Newton and Mowbray area. It was handier for me at Holme St Cuthbert's, as a bus went round that way and I didn't need to bike from Allonby. There were two teachers and it was a lovely, lovely school. I had a classroom with a piano to myself, and I got a washbasin put in the room so the kiddies could wash their hands. Mr Fawcett was the head of the school and he retired when I did. I retired when I was sixty and still had an active life, reading, knitting and biking. I enjoyed all my years teaching and had a lot of fun being sent to other schools.

There was little or no changes in teaching from when I started school until I retired but I don't think that continued for long. Oh, we don't agree with the modern teaching. You should see the children's three Rs. There's a lot of poor teaching and I think parents have a lot to do with it, they should help their children. One thing that has changed is that years ago, when youngsters left school, boys usually went into farm work and the girls went into service. That's a change for the better.

Out of the forty years that I taught, there was less than ten children who I could not teach to read. Of the rest, some might have been slow but they could read, even if it was only comics. Only one parent ever came to see me and I'll tell you what happened. They used pen and ink in those days and this child made a mess and did some awful work. I said, 'That's awful, I'm not going to have that work', and I smacked him on his shoulder. He was given another piece of paper and made to do the work again, which he did beautifully. His mother came to see me later and I said, 'Come and see what he did.' I showed her both sets of her son's work and she agreed with me. That boy passed his scholarship.

I should think I'm the oldest woman left from Allonby. The mill has gone, nearly everybody from my childhood has gone, and when I go that will be the end of the old times at Allonby. I still keep in touch with my relations in Canada and supply them with information about the family and have been four times to see them. I can't read much now and, oh, I used to read such a lot. When I had my stroke my speech was sort of slurred. I had to think of the words and I was annoyed when I wanted to say something and I knew I couldn't. But my memory hasn't gone at all and my speech is coming back. I've told you all this, haven't I?

FIVE

'Whisky was eightpence a tot'

EDNA (b. 1920)
Hassness/Buttermere/Loweswater

My dad came from the Wigton area originally. He was from a big family. I think there would be about thirteen of them and most went into mining. I remember going with Dad to visit his sister who lived at Crosby Villa. We cycled to Cockermouth where we got the train to Bullgill and then walked to Crosby Villa. I was amazed when the miners came home from the pits. Dad's sister had a big tin bath in front of the fire. Her family came in and stripped everything off, no matter who was in. Then they got into the bath, one after another, and had this huge meal waiting for them when they got out. Now they'd have baths at the pit head and go home clean – if there was any pits left.

I was born in 1920 at Papcastle but I was only about two years old when we left and went to live at Hassness, near Buttermere. Dad got a job as a gardener for a Mr O'Hanlon who was a manufacturer from

Edna as a baby

Manchester. Mr O'Hanlon had a big house and employed three women who worked indoors and three gardeners outside. He never actually lived at Hassness permanently. It was just a holiday home for him.

It was a mile out of Buttermere was Hassness. We lived in just a tiny cottage which had a kitchen, living room and back kitchen, and upstairs were two bedrooms. The loo was across the yard. I think we had an oil stove in the back kitchen that Mother would cook on and of course there was a fireside range in the living room. For light there was candles and oil lamps. Nearby were two cottages but there was no other children for me to play with.

I walked the mile to Buttermere School and my brother also did when he was old enough to attend. Not far from our cottage, on the lake edge, there was a boat. When it was really fine weather Mother used to tie my brother and me in the boat and row us down the lake to the school. But we had to be tied in, as my brother was very small at that time. Our teacher, Mrs Beattie, travelled from Lorton, and later on from Isel, every day on a motorbike. Oh, I liked Buttermere School. I think we all got individual attention, you know, as there were never very many of us – only about ten or twelve pupils in one big room. We were allowed to play in the field behind the school but mostly played on the rocks between the church and the river. I didn't take sandwiches to school as my grandparents' farm was near and I used to go there for lunch.

We had to go to Sunday School every Sunday. This was always before the church service and we stayed until the second hymn of the service before we came out of church. We were dressed up for Sunday and always got a new dress for Easter and used to go to church to show it off. Then we'd go for a walk in the afternoon and roll our pasche eggs [hard-boiled eggs prepared for Easter] down Hartley Hill.

In summer as children we used to go down to the lake and paddle and play about. The hotels mostly owned their own boats which were looked after by a boatman. It was mostly people staying in the village who used the lake for fishing. There was char in Crummock Water and nets were weighted down and dropped into the lake to catch them.

I spent a lot of my time at my grandparents' farm in the village and I can remember sitting there in the winter, cutting rags up from old clothes to make hookie mats. The frames were brought out and we all used to sit around and prod and hook the mats. Grandad was a lovely old man who farmed with two of his sons. Another two sons and their wives ran the other farm he rented at Seatoller. I sometimes used to go over there for my school holidays, walking from Buttermere over Honister Pass on my own. Most times I never saw anyone on the way – only the men working in the quarries. My grandmother was very smart, with a little piece of velvet round her neck. She always wore a blouse, long black skirt and apron. To me, she was a really old lady, but she wasn't terribly old when she died.

I was only about eight when Grandma died and we moved down to the farm so that Mother could help out. We still had the cottage and went backwards and forwards but mostly stayed on the farm. Besides visitors who stayed at the farm, four-in-hand coaches came over Honister Pass and stopped for tea. These coaches used to come from Keswick and the passengers would have their lunch at the Buttermere Hotel. They'd go for a walk in the afternoon and come to the farm for their tea before their return journey to Keswick over Newlands. On the wall of the farm was the initials CTC which stood for the Cyclists Touring Club as their members also used to come and stay.

The farm could take up to eight or nine visitors at a time and they usually came by train to Cockermouth Station where they'd be met by taxi. Visitors mostly went walking or climbing and would be out all day, coming back for dinner at night. Or sometimes they might take their sandwiches, get a boat and row across to the islands on Crummock Water. If they didn't want to take sandwiches, they had lunch in and afternoon tea. The visitors' season was from Easter till about September. We always reckoned that the last spell of visitors was for Loweswater Show about the middle of September.

Visitors from Edna's grandparents' farm, 'dressed up' on a visit to Haigh Pit, 1920s

The Loweswater Show was much the same as it is today. From school we used to enter drawings, writing and wild flowers that we picked. My mother and her sisters did quite a lot of baking for the show. I remember them baking cornflour cakes, which were very dodgy to make as they used to drop as soon as you took them out of the oven. We were eating cornflour cakes for weeks until Mother got them fit to take to the show.

There was one old chap, a tramp called Tommy Denwood, who used to come to the farm. He slept in the loft in the barn and my grandfather used to go up and empty Tommy's pockets of any matches that he had. Then Tommy would be covered in hay, and wooden posts put on top to keep him warm and for a bit of weight. Next morning Tommy would be given a bacon sandwich when he came with an old can for his tea. The farm was one of Tommy's regular calling places but what happened to him we never knew. On the way to Buttermere were quite a number of gates where tramps used to stand. They'd open the gates when the four-in-hands were approaching and all the passengers used to throw money on to the road for them to collect.

I was eleven when my parents took over the Kirkstile Inn at Loweswater, as they wanted a place of their own. I'll always remember the day we moved. The coalman loaned us his big wagon for the day and what we couldn't get on we put on the block cart. I travelled on the block cart, our horse, Maggie, was in front and there was a space for me to sit so that I could open the gates along the way.

At that time there was a school, a blacksmith's, a joiner's and a sweetshop at Loweswater but they've all gone now. The blacksmith's did a good trade because it was all horses then, there were no tractors. A chap called Johnston, who lived at Lorton, had the blacksmith's at both Lorton and Loweswater, doing so many days in each place. For the sweetshop, you went into a little cottage which had a table to the right and a piano on the left. Only sweets were sold – aniseed balls, toffees, all the usual old-fashioned types.

An old wooden army hut stood in a corner of a nearby field. That was our village hall which we used for dances. Farm lads went there at nights to play pool, dominoes or sit round the stove and talk. There was one old chap who worked on a farm and he would do anything for an ounce of baccy for his pipe. If there was a dance at the hall, or if they were making suppers there, he would carry buckets of water from the inn to the hall. His baccy was his pay for the night. The Mothers Union and Girls Friendly Society were held at the church opposite us. The church also had a choir and all the young ones were in the choir in those days, whether they could sing or not.

Loweswater Smithy, 1920s

When we first moved to the Kirkstile, Loweswater School had just closed for the children over eleven and we were supposed to go to Cockermouth School by bus. But parents didn't want their children to go to Cockermouth and a strike was on. So we'd present ourselves at Loweswater School in the morning and the teacher would send us home. That went on for a long while and my parents decided to send me back to Buttermere School because I was missing so much education.

On a Sunday night after tea I'd set off with my week's pocket money and get fifty aniseed balls with my penny at the village shop, which was my ration for the week. Then I walked through Lanthwaite Woods back to Buttermere and stayed with an aunt and uncle for the week while I went to school. On Friday night the greengrocer went to Buttermere before calling at Loweswater and he'd collect me from school and bring me home. There was supposed to be a ghost in Lanthwaite Woods but what it was I don't know. It never bothered me, walking on my own the four miles to Buttermere. Eventually the strike got settled and we had to start Cockermouth School. It was a bit of a shock to me, being used to a little school and then coming into town, into this big school.

The school bus took about half an hour to reach Cockermouth. As children we had never been to Cockermouth very much, though Mother used to go to town for her shopping. Our teacher was very keen on Cockermouth Carnival and used to help us get dressed up for it – it was a big day out. The procession and floats went up Lorton Street, down the Main Street, and down to the bottom of the town where we used to gather at a huge field. We'd get a paper bag with a bun or little things like a biscuit or sweets and join the parade.

The Kirkstile Inn was a farm then, with outbuildings in the yard. It was still like that when we left twenty-five years later. Where the bar is now was our cow shed. Dad paid the rent on the property twice a year, at Candlemas and then in the autumn. He used to go to the Globe Hotel at Cockermouth and a firm of solicitors used to come there and collect the rents. At first my dad managed the farm on his own, until my brother was old enough to work. But we would go out and help him at busy times, with the hay-making, milking and suchlike.

The yard at the Kirkstile Inn, 1920s

We had no indoor sanitation. The toilets were a long way down the yard, and round the garden there was two which were back to back. Also in the yard was a pump, which was our only supply of water. Inside, there was a big old-fashioned range in the kitchen and a little bar with seats all round where the men sat drinking. So Mother had to do her cooking on this range, in front of them all. Now this range had a huge frying pan, which hung on a hook over the fire, and you were able to get a dozen eggs in the pan for ham and egg teas. The side boiler took about six buckets of water, which we had to fill every morning, and that was our only means of heating water.

It used to take about an hour to clean the whole range and that was a job, using brushes, blacklead and brasso. Every morning the blue-flagged floor and white-topped tables were scrubbed. And in the afternoon the floor was done over again with a mop. As children we weren't allowed to go into the rooms where the men were drinking. We had to go and sit upstairs in our rooms and play dominoes or cards.

For the visitors we had a dining room, with three big tables, which opened out on to the small sitting room. In the visitors' bedrooms were washbasins and chamber pots, as we didn't have a bathroom to begin with. We had to take big jugs of hot water up every morning for them to wash with and then the slops were carried down. When we first moved in, there was five bedrooms but after a few years we altered the stable and made it into a kitchen and put the bathroom and a couple of single bedrooms above.

I always wanted to be a nurse but when I left school at fourteen I stayed at home and helped my mother. At first I wasn't allowed to work in the bar as I was too young. So I waited on the visitors and Mother showed me how to do the cooking and suchlike. Monday was washing day and the washing would be hung up on a pulley at night in the kitchen or else we could hang it in the barn where there was a through-draught. Tuesday was for ironing, churning day was Wednesday, Thursday was for any extra little bits of cleaning and Friday was baking day. Saturday was a real turn-out day because nearly all the guests came and eventually left on that day, so it was busy.

In summer it was hot and dusty. So before you started to sweep, and to keep the dust from rising, you soaked newpapers in water. The water was squeezed out and the paper torn into little pieces which were scattered over the bedroom floor to collect the dust. There was no hoovers and you had to get down on your hands and knees with a brush and shovel to sweep the bedrooms out. Then there was the oil lamps to trim every morning and fill up with oil ready for night. We never had electricity all the years that I lived at the inn.

Farmers joined together for most things like clipping, hay-making and harvest time. Each farm had a threshing day when the thresher came round. Then the farmer's wife would make tatie pot and rice pudding for everybody who was helping. All the farms had their own piece of fell for the sheep to go on to, and if they were brought up there the sheep would stick to it. The farmers would go up on to the fellside and cut bracken which was used as bedding for the cattle. The bracken was cut and left for a while to dry out and then a sledge was taken up the fell to collect it.

One year when I was little, Dad found a tent up on the fell with all the cooking utensils, a little stove and everything. There was a label attached to the tent that read, 'The finder may keep this, as we are too tired to carry it any further.' So Dad brought the tent and everything home and we had a great time with it. Strangely enough we didn't have many bad winters until '47. That year, a neighbour and Dad went up on the fell and found a whole lot of sheep hidden behind a wall. The sheep were covered in snow but they were still alive. Dad had some little bottles of brandy in his pocket to give the sheep a tot and warm them through.

Every farm kept pigs and had a pig-killing day. My uncle used to butch ours and he used to say that you can use every part of a pig except its squeal. When we were butching, his wife came to help my mother. One of her jobs was to stir the blood for the black puddings and she learnt me that. We used to fill the big boiler in the wash-house, and once the pig was dead we poured boiling water over it and my uncle scraped all the hair off. Other folk used a knife but my uncle used an old sharp candlestick that he kept just for that job. When meat was cut, it was hung up for the night in the barn doorway to cool. You couldn't do that today – it would be gone next morning. After the meat was cut up and salted, it was brought into the house and hung up on big hooks all round the kitchen to dry. Then we had our black puddings and sausage to make, and if you had a lot of sausage it used to go out to various families in the village. When they butched, they brought us some to share. Nothing tastes the same today as it did then.

In those days it was mostly locals who came to the inn because there wasn't the cars. It was just anyone who could walk or come on a bike but no women came in for a drink, no women at all. On a Monday, the regulars would call on their way back from Cockermouth Market. Either they'd have cycled to Cockermouth, used the school bus or got a lift back with the big wagons that had taken their stock to market. Then they'd smoke, play dominoes and sometimes have a sing-song.

We used to have lots of old gentlemen as regulars and they all had their own seat. They weren't a bit suited if they came in and anybody else was sitting in their seat. These elderly men wore corduroy trousers and often wrapped hessian bags tied with twine around their legs to keep warm. On their flat caps there'd be more hessian made into a peak at the front and hanging down the back of their neck. Usually they wore a muffler and smoked a clay pipe or cigarettes. The cigarettes were sixpence for a packet of ten Capstan, Goldflake or Players. Woodbines were fourpence. In those days we had the old metal spitoons which we had to empty and fill up with sawdust every morning. That was one job I didn't like. Not a bit hygienic, was it?

The Kirkstile was a free house and we could get our drink from wherever we wanted. Draught beer was the most popular drink and we had Younger's beer but mostly it was Jennings from Cockermouth. The traveller from the brewery came round for our order, the beer was delivered by lorry into the cellar and the draymen always got a pint. Jefferson's of Whitehaven used to supply us with the sherry and we got whisky from Jimmy Dixon in Cockermouth.

I remember when I was first learning the trade a bottle of Guinness was eightpence and a half-size baby Guinness was fourpence. Whisky was eightpence a tot and twelve shillings and sixpence a bottle. You could buy either a bottle of sherry or port for six shillings, and a glass of draught beer was threepence. When customers gave you their order the beer was pulled from the barrel into a big jug, then you filled the glasses from the jug and carried it on a tray to their table. People didn't drink a lot in those days because they couldn't afford it, they hadn't the money.

For visitors, bed and breakfast was five shillings when we first started. A full breakfast was bacon, egg, sausage, black pudding and tomatoes – a real plateful. Full board was the big breakfast, sandwiches at lunchtime and then afternoon or ham and egg tea. Tea consisted of ham and two eggs, brown and white bread and butter, fruit bread, scones, jam and rum butter, cake, pastry and a variety of small cakes. Full board was seven shillings and sixpence, while the afternoon tea on its own was two shillings and sixpence. After we'd been at the inn for a while, Brown's coaches from Ambleside used to come round by Wastwater for lunch and then the Kirkstile for tea. So we'd do pots of tea, tea and scones, full afternoon tea or ham and egg teas.

Towards Christmastime there would be domino competitions and always bottles and suchlike for prizes. Christmas Day we spent on our own – it was a family time. We weren't closed but families more or less stayed at home that day. New Year's Eve was hilarious, we were doing all sorts of things. We would pick up a wheelbarrow at one farm, take it up to the next, then pick their wheelbarrow up and so on. Everybody was looking for their wheelbarrow the following morning.

Melbreak Fox Hounds used to meet at the Kirkstile on New Year's Day and that was a busy time. The Melbreak Hunt always had their Opening Meet there as well and we'd make big potato pots, plum pudding and apple pie and cream, with the huntsmen getting a pint of beer to go with it. Farmers were bothered by foxes then just as they are today. During the lambing season if there were any dead lambs they used to send for the hounds for an early morning hunt to catch Reynard. Nowadays, because of all this drink and drive business, people can't stay and have a drink. And a lot of the hunters come in cars. They don't walk or cycle now and it means they go straight home again. There isn't the gatherings like there used to be.

In winter, from September to Easter, we used to do our decorating. There was painting and wallpapering to do, and we had to make rugs, do our knitting and still run the farm. The Women's Institute was held in the village hall, which my mother joined when it first started and I joined later. Eventually we got a dramatic society and I joined that as well. We used to do either a three-act play or three one-act plays in the village hall and then these were taken round the surrounding villages. We had lots of fun with that.

As teenagers, we used to cycle to dances at Lorton, Lamplugh, Ennerdale, Braithwaite, the Drill Hall at Cockermouth and even the Princess Hall at Workington once or twice. The neighbouring village dances didn't start until about ten o'clock and finished about three in the morning. I also used to cycle into Cockermouth for shopping. I'd fasten a basket on to the back of the bike, another one to the front and that way I could get quite a bit of shopping. We always needed to go into town to buy fresh yeast for making our own bread. Anything else we needed to buy, even clothes, we mostly bought from the travelling vans that came round. The salesmen carried suitcases, which they opened and spread all their goods on the floor. You ordered what you wanted and then it was delivered later.

The war made a difference, especially with the visitors and the rationing. We weren't allowed much, so it was a struggle really. Some things we had to do without. We had to cut out ham and egg teas and things like that because we just didn't have the food to go round. My brother was working on another farm and was in the Home Guard in the village. I was exempt because of helping on the farm and at the inn but they were hard times.

I married when I was twenty-seven and Mother made our wedding reception at home. My husband-to-be was in the Army all during the war and I met him again when he came out of the forces. That year the school at Loweswater closed down altogether, so we got the flat above the school as it wasn't used. Later, when we moved to a little house down the village, the school was extended and altered for meetings. My husband worked for the Forestry Commission and he travelled by pushbike every morning from Loweswater to Whinlatter Pass before we eventually managed to get a motorbike. I still went to the Kirkstile every day to help, but when my father died, Mother retired. Then I looked for something else to do, as I've always kept busy.

I started doing bed and breakfast and put a sign outside our house. If other people in the same trade were full they would recommend one

Edna feeding sheep outside the Kirkstile Inn, 1930s

another. That's how you started. And the same way doing teas – you just
stuck a notice in the garden saying 'Teas'. I did a real Cumberland tea – a
plate of white and brown bread, fruit malt, scones, rum butter and jam.
There was always a fruit cake (or fruit loaf as we called it), sponges,
gingerbread, a dish of fancy cakes and a fruit pie. When I first started it
was one shilling and ninepence for a tea and it was about £1 when I
stopped seven years ago. But it costs much more now – it's about £3
when you go out for a meal like that. I enjoyed cooking. I think, in that
line of business, you've got to enjoy it.

There wasn't much bed and breakfast trade at first but it gradually
built up and people started coming back. A lot of the regulars were from
the Manchester area but I had lots from abroad. There were Canadians,
Australians and Americans, but some of the Americans I didn't like as
they used to take the place over. I still get a postcard from a couple of
Americans who used to stay with me. They used to bring their cycles
over to England in pieces, put them together when they landed and use
them all the time they were here. Later, when I moved, I brought the
garden seat with me. One day I was out shopping and when I came back
there was two bicycles at the end of the drive. When I went round the
back, there were these two Americans sitting on the seat. They said, 'We
knew it was your house because we recognised the seat.'

Nearly all the farms did bed and breakfast and no one came round and inspected the premises. In those days you only applied for permission if you wanted to put a board out on the roadside. In winter we did our painting, decorating, knitting, repairing things and mending sheets. With old sheets, we took them to pieces, cut the best bits out and made pillow slips out of them. You socialised a bit too, as you had no time in the summer.

I didn't learn to drive until I was about fifty. My daughter was at grammar school and began wanting to stay on for things at night, after school. Well, with starting work early, my husband went to bed early and didn't like turning out at night. So I decided that I would learn to drive and he said, 'You'll never pass the test.' Well, that was like a red rag to a bull. I prepared my visitors' breakfasts in the morning, caught the bus to Cockermouth, another bus to Workington and had an hour's driving lesson. Then I got the bus back to Cockermouth, did some shopping and caught the school bus home at four o'clock. Some weeks I missed my lesson when I was busy but I started in February and passed my test in October. It was a good help once I'd learnt to drive. I could go into town and do my own shopping.

I moved nearer the town when I was past retirement age and it took me about twelve months to settle down, with being used to the country. Today I can go back to the village and, apart from a few people, they're all strangers to me. Such a lot of the farms have been sold off. The houses and land have been let privately, they're not little farms any more. I don't approve of it – all these little farms being split up and so many holiday homes. Once you knew everybody and could go out for a walk, open anybody's door and go in. It's all gone now and I'm glad I lived in that area when I did. I wouldn't have liked to live anywhere else.

SIX

'Folk were glad of jobs in them days'

∽

DOROTHY ELLISON (b. 1905)
Workington/Barrow

I was born at 6 Brow Top, Workington, in June 1905. These were just small houses that looked right down onto the Cloffocks and the River Derwent. There were eight children – two sisters and a brother older than me and the rest younger. I've a younger sister and two younger brothers left. I've lived to be the oldest so I must have been the toughest.

Dad was a cycle-maker from Cockermouth originally. He went to a private school there when he was young and his sisters went to Miss Todd's Academy for Young Ladies. My mother was from Broughton way, where her family were miners. Little Broughton was where my great-great-grandmother lived but all I can remember of her is a little old lady sitting in a corner, who was nice to talk to. And my great-grandmother from Great Broughton emigrated to Canada. I don't know anything more about her. We once went to the cemetery at Little Broughton to look for a family grave, and there were so many head-stones with my mother's maiden name we must have been interbred!

I don't remember much about Workington at this time but I know there was a Shopping Week. That was when all the shops and streets used to be decorated to get tourists into town and there was a procession and a band. I'd started at St John's School in Workington but we moved to Barrow when I was six years old. My eldest sister stayed at Broughton with Grandma. I think she'd probably gone to Grandma's when one of the younger kiddies had been born and just stayed there.

We moved to Anchor Road on Barrow Island so that Dad could get a job at the shipyard. Things were starting to be bad then and the war came a few years afterwards. Two of Dad's brothers and their families already lived in Barrow. They had come to work in the yard, so there was quite a lot of us really. We were always in touch with each other and saw most of the family every day, which was good. Lots of people travelled in daily to the shipyard by train from Ulverston and Dalton way. Others came and settled in Barrow for the work, as we had.

Dorothy's great-grandmother who emigrated to Canada

There was a lot of tenements around and houses were being built for all the people coming into the town. I can't remember any nastiness among the neighbours. Everyone was nice and friendly – they didn't need to lock their doors. If there was any trouble the neighbours always tried to help each other or see if there was anything they could do. Our next-door neighbour was fond of children and if she was ever going out she always came and took one of our babies with her. She wrapped the baby close to her with a shawl she wore over her shoulders. Women usually did wear shawls then, over their coats.

Dad worked long hours at the shipyard, especially when the First World War came. Normally he started work at six in the morning and came home for his breakfast at half-past eight, as we lived near the shipyard. Then he came home at twelve o'clock for his dinner and he finished work at six o'clock. He would have a drink at weekends, as most men did, but no one was nasty with drink. If you saw someone drunk, you would always say to them, 'Come on, it's time you were home.'

Funnily enough, the school I started at Barrow was also called St John's. It was just over the road from where we lived and was a very good school. The teachers were nice and kept you fairly well in place. I remember a new teacher starting and she banged on the table, told us her name and said, 'I'm here to teach you and I'll reprimand you as well', holding up the cane. Another teacher, Miss Buchanan, said she wanted a class that she didn't have to cane. We all got through the year without being caned, as she was a nice teacher and knew how to handle children. Of course you didn't dare get out of line in those days, like they do now. You had to do as you were told – you were brought up to.

For school I wore a dress in summer and a kilt and jersey in winter. Underneath we wore a liberty bodice and a vest if it was cold. Elasticated knickers hadn't come in then. It was cotton bloomers with lace around the bottom that fastened with buttons at the waist. I've worn clogs in winter and they were warm and it was nice having cawkers [steel rims] on them because you could go along the pavement and kick to make sparks. Then you got into trouble for wearing the cawkers out.

The Sunday School was part of the day school and the church was right next door. The worst part of going to Sunday School was that when you came out they used to lead you right into church. We didn't like that because we had Sunday School in the afternoon as well. My mother never minded us going to both places, as I dare say she was glad of a bit of peace when we were out of the road. Everybody went to Sunday School in those days and we had a Sunday School trip once a year. We went by train and marched up like a little army to the station, to go to Greenodd or somewhere similar. Tea, sandwiches and cakes were provided.

As children we played on Walney shore or at Furness Abbey. Going round the abbey was free and nobody did any damage. At Barrow there was what was called the Timber Pond. In this pond was a lot of wooden sleepers getting ready for use. I don't know why they were put in the pond but we used to go on them. You do daft things. We used to jump on these sleepers and swing about until the water was coming over the edge of the wood. I fell in once and, oh, it was deep. My legs got tangled underneath and I don't know how I managed to get out. I was coming home crying when a man asked what was wrong. When I told him he said it served me right. I did get my bottom smacked when I got home because we had been playing tig on the sleepers, which we shouldn't have been.

The Timber Pond was near where all the cargo ships came in and there was a big green where all the children played. Some of the dago men used to come off the ships but there was never any trouble. I know some fellas off the ships used to go round the houses and sell Spanish onions, which were good and cheap.

As kiddies, we used to shout 'More money, more pennies' when people got married and money would be thrown on to the street for us. When a couple got married from a big block of flats in Barrow the kiddies were down below shouting and the money was coming out of the window. But the kiddies went on shouting so long that somebody eventually threw water down on to them!

Being a big family, we all worked together and my father helped out. When you were bathed at night, the tin bath was brought out and Dad would get the children ready for bed. He was good that way and did the washing up. Dad never smacked me in his life, but he looked so stern you did as you were told. If Dad was at home when mother was in labour, he used to look after us kiddies downstairs while everything was going on upstairs. The old midwife used to come in a hurry then, with her shawl around her, but as children we were always kept out of the way. I remember we had a wooden cradle on rockers but I don't think it got rocked much. It was never brought downstairs because there wasn't the room with all the family. Whether this cradle was hired I don't know, but it just appeared for each baby.

Mother worked hard. She did her own baking and washing, of course. But when I was quite young I had to do a lot of the shopping. You started doing the shopping when you were six or seven in those days. I was the one who seemed to be able to do it, I don't know why. We shopped at the Co-op, which was just a little way from where we lived. It was a butcher's, grocer's and draper's all together so I got most of the shopping there.

Before the First World War started I saw a zeppelin going over Barrow. Later we wondered if it had been taking photos of the shipyard. When the war did begin, soldiers were stationed in barracks at the school. One day a few of us kiddies were playing with a ball near this school when a soldier asked if they could borrow it to have a kick around with. When they'd finished playing with it the soldier asked our names, and when I told him mine it turned out that he was a relation of Dad's from West Cumberland. So when he was able, he came across to our house to visit us and have a talk with Dad.

As kiddies, we used to watch the soldiers marching up and down the street and we'd cheer them on. At school we knitted scarves and squares for blankets for the war effort, and when the war finished everybody nearly went mad. I don't think anybody could settle down because they were so excited. The schoolchildren had a party but a lot of people waited until their men came home before they had their celebrations.

During the First World War we had to queue for goods – margarine especially – and then I'd go up to the Maypole to see what I could buy. I remember once going to the Maypole and they had a big policeman on the door who only let so many people into the shop at a time. When I got to the head of the queue he said, 'Now, that's enough, you'll all have to wait until they've had their dinner.' Well, that meant I would have stood outside for another hour and I was only about ten years old. This policeman was standing with his legs apart, so I scrambled between his legs and got into the shop before they closed the doors. He couldn't do anything about it as the crowd were killing themselves laughing. You had to do those sort of things. Life wasn't easy. Women had a very hard time – they had big families and there was very little money around.

There was no National Health in those days and you couldn't really afford to send for the doctor. The only times I can remember the doctor being sent for was when my younger brothers and sisters had measles, all at the same time. Also my younger sister had bronchial asthma and she sounded at times as if she was going to choke. At times like that the doctor came. Asthma was terrible and the only thing that seemed to do my sister any good was ipicacuana wine. I used to go to the chemist and buy two-pennyworth of this wine and I had a terrible job remembering how to say 'ipicacuana' at first.

At eleven years old I had the chance of sitting an exam and going to the higher grade, which was not far from the Town Hall. But it was no good me going in for it because an auntie said that my mother wouldn't be able to buy the uniform and books, not with having the rest of the family. I was three months off my fourteenth birthday when I was allowed to leave school, as I got an exemption. That was because my aunt at Workington was waiting for me to go and work with her. I was in the top class at school and the top girl so I wasn't losing anything by leaving.

My aunt and uncle had a plumbing business on Oxford Street in Workington and it was as clean as any confectioner's shop. The floor was polished and everything was scrupulously clean. They had three or four men working for them because there was a housing scheme at the time. A terrible lot of new houses were being built and my uncle was doing the plumbing for nearly all of them. The workmen came to the door at eight o'clock, so we had to have breakfast over by then. My auntie and me did

Oxford Street, Workington, 1930s

the housework and looked after the shop between us, but sometimes at spring-cleaning she got a relation in to help.

My first wage was only five bob but, mind, it wasn't like working for anybody else. Anything I wanted in the clothes line was given to me. Folk were glad of jobs in them days – there wasn't always jobs even for men. I remember once going out for a walk in Workington and I met somebody I knew. She was working for a bank clerk's wife as a servant – a bank clerk's wife, not a bank manager's wife – so what wage this girl got I don't know, but she wouldn't have got much.

Barrow and Workington were similar in some ways and, oh, the people were very, very poor and in a bad way. It was terrible, and the poverty was unbelievable. I've seen kiddies going to school in rags and with nothing on their feet. I'm sure the poverty was worse in Workington but there was soup kitchens in both towns. There was a lot of tramps but they weren't allowed into the shops because you never knew if they were going to pick anything up from the shop.

All towns had workhouses and Barrow had a big one. That's where a lot of old people went if they hadn't the money or families to look after them. You see, after the First World War there was such a lot of poverty because there was so many people out of work. I remember my dad being out of work at the shipyard for a long time. My parents had to sell a lot of things to keep going, just as most people had to. Then gradually the shipyard got back on its feet, which was a good thing, as it was that yard and the steelworks that kept Barrow going.

And it wasn't just food that people were short of money for. When there was a death, and they couldn't afford a hearse, they had to carry the coffin. If they had a bit of money there would be a hearse and maybe just one pony and trap. The more money they had, the more ponies and traps.

If people had a decent piece of clothing, it was kept for Sunday. You had to be careful of your clothes and keep them clean and tidy, that was the main thing. I was lucky, as a relation was a very good dressmaker, so I got things made cheap and had a few more than if I'd had to buy them. My auntie was good to my mother and sent her things to help out. Now people think they are poor when they can't afford luxuries.

One person I can remember at Workington was old 'Darkie Joe' who lived down Church Street way. He was a big, tall, coloured man, always smiling, and a bit of a worker as well. There was no racial discrimination at all but there was discrimination between the Catholics and the Protestants, even for jobs. If it was a Catholic firm a Catholic got the job before the Protestant and vice versa. There was a bit of a hatred between the two religions. Whether it was just a certain class of people that got worked up, I don't know. Thankfully that's all gone now.

'Darkie Joe', 1905

In my free time I went to the pictures when I could afford it. Most people in Workington went for walks in them days, especially on a Sunday, as there wasn't the money for anything else. They liked walking and you always used to meet somebody you knew. Families all went out together on a Sunday, children and parents. It was the one time they could get together because men worked such long hours on other days. Round the Shore Hills was a lovely walk, along the Mill Field, the poor-

Workington Hall, 1930

house, Stainburn Road and Cuckoo Arch, Workington Hall and Camerton – oh they were all lovely walks. I wasn't allowed out every night, even though it was my auntie I worked for, and I had to be in by nine at night. Later, I even had a job going to the Princess Hall Dance. I could only go when my cousins were playing in the band there.

I used to go to the PSA, which was the 'Pleasant Sunday Afternoon'. This was held in the Hippodrome and lasted about an hour and a half. An orchestra played hymns and a march, nothing that would upset anybody who was really religious. Then there'd be a sermon, we sang another hymn and the orchestra played again while they came round with the collection. Later in the evening it was either church or a long walk with girl friends, seeing if you could talk to the boys and get off with them.

While I was away from home, my younger sister died at Barrow. She was only sixteen and had consumption. A terrible lot of people got it in those days and they were sent to a sanatorium. Although my sister's consumption was advanced, and a doctor attended her, she stayed at home. Some people did recover from consumption but I never heard of anybody who was completely strong again. Whether it was because they were pampered because they'd had the illness, I don't know.

My mum managed to come through to see me sometimes and it was nice to see her. Of course she came to see my elder sister and grandparents as well at Broughton. Grandad's house was fairly big and had a big back garden. Up in the country, at Broughton, they had ash closets, as they used to be called, which were in the garden and had two seats – a big one for grown-ups and a small one for children.

My mother's dad was a deputy in the mines. I can't remember which one, as there was quite a few mines around and I know even Annie Pit was still working then. Grandad was a character, very much to the point in a lot of things. Sometimes when you thought he was being stern you could see the twinkle in his eye. Even though I was only fourteen, as I was working, he treated me as an adult. He wouldn't let you sit down with just a cup of tea if everybody else was having a meal. You had to have your meal set out properly like him. When you got a few miners talking together outside, they always used to sit on their heels, crouched down, because they worked such a lot that way in the pits. In town we used to see the young ones who'd started in the mines going to and from work. They always seemed happy but people round that way were a good lot of folk to work with.

Most men worked at the mines or the steelworks. When they tipped the slag from the steelworks it lit the sky up at night. The sky got lovely and rosy and we noticed it more because streets weren't lit as well as they are now. Street lights went out at a certain time during the night and you could see from the bedroom window when the slag came out – all the sky would light up beautifully.

My elder sister at Broughton married and went to live in Manchester. I decided to go and live with her, and got a job as a nurse. I was there about a year but I wanted to come back to Workington. My auntie came to see us and she asked me to have my old job again and I did. I was glad to come back and be near all my relations.

Funnily enough, I met my future husband at my auntie's. A friend of the family had left his motorbike in the warehouse at the bottom of the yard. This motorbike had broken down and he brought a chap to have a look at it. Well, while this chap was mending the bike, we met and fancied each other. My husband came from Princess Street in Workington but was working at Cockermouth as a motor mechanic. The company he was working for were facing a bad time and he wasn't sure if he was going to be kept on, so he came to Kendal and got work. And it was a good job he got as a motor mechanic – his wage was £5 a week.

I was twenty-three when we got married and we had a quiet wedding, as I didn't want anything else. That was all I wanted because it was all we could afford. We married at eight o'clock in the morning and besides my auntie and uncle, who gave me away, there was only a bridesmaid and best man. We went to Blackpool on my husband's motorbike for our honeymoon and stayed in a boarding house. It was a very good place to stay. We were happy, got good meals and didn't get into debt.

As my husband was working at Kendal, we got rooms at first, then moved into a flat. Eventually we got a proper little house, then saved enough money for a deposit on this one. It was scratching and saving all the time.

By this time my husband was a partner in the garage, but when war broke out this partner, who was in the Reserves, was called up. So I had to go to the garage, was shown how to do the book-keeping and got that job during the war. It had to be done properly but it was one of those double-entry affairs and easy to follow.

Having a garage was not like having a grocer's shop during the war – people didn't have to register with us. Anyone could come for petrol as long as they had petrol coupons. And we had to have the coupons for our next load of petrol. How many coupons people had depended on how many gallons they were allowed, and it wouldn't be a big amount, just a few gallons a month. Mostly, it was businesspeople or reps who got more petrol and they had to be careful with what they got. Very few people had cars in those days so really it was just small businesses and wagons.

We were kept going and had to stay open at certain hours and closed at half-past seven during the week. When there was the blackout we had to close earlier. But even towards the end of the war we were open on Sundays as well, until two o'clock in the afternoon. The work was there because there was no new cars – the old ones just had to be repaired.

When the war finished and the partner came back I retired from the job for a while. It was just as well I did because I found I was expecting. I thought I couldn't have children, as when we first married I just didn't have any. I never bothered after that – I just thought it wasn't to be. Then, after sixteen years of married life, I started being sick in the mornings. I waited quite a while before I saw the doctor, who confirmed I was pregnant and we were delighted. So it was in 1947 that I had my only child, a boy. But in those days you weren't given advice or told to rest, you just carried on working.

After the war, when petrol wasn't rationed, one of the best weeks we ever used to have was when the Scottish holidays were on. You see, there was no motorway and all the traffic came through town. The Scots were good payers and nearly always gave a tip to whoever was serving petrol. Sometimes you were run off your feet. I'd be busy doing the books and my husband would shout up from the garage, 'Can you come and serve? We're too busy in the garage.'

I've worked most of my life, as most people had to. If you wanted to live, you had to work. People talk about the poverty today but it's nothing compared to what there used to be. And, no, I wouldn't wish those days back again, I really wouldn't.

SEVEN

'Thursday night was the Ladies Circle'

RITA GROAT (b. 1910)
Kendal

My father was from the Orkney Islands and went to train as a medical student at Edinburgh University Hospital. Unfortunately he caught measles and his sight was so impaired that he couldn't go on with his training. He then came to England where he trained at a Nottingham college and became a clergyman. After my father married my mother he was a minister at Melrose and Gateshead, before coming to Kendal in 1907 as minister for the Zion Congregational Chapel.

I was born in 1910 at 4 Queen's Place, Kendal. We didn't live in a church house, as my father, being very independent, rented a house. I had one sister, Mildred, who was fourteen years older than me and was at boarding school. When she came home she was more like a second mother to me. I adored her – she used to read to me for hours and hours.

My earliest memories are of playing in a great big field near my home. This was owned by the uncle of a little friend who lived next door but one. We were allowed to play in the field until one dreadful day. In a fit of madness, which attacks young children when they're being naughty, we threw sacks and sacks of corn feed to the hens. We weren't allowed to go there again.

Very few people had telephones in those days. On Queen's Road lived the Somervilles who were great friends of my father's. Someone rang Mr Somerville from London to tell him that war had broken out, so he came straight across to our house to tell Dad. Dad looked out of the window and saw two of his neighbours playing quoits in the 'infamous' field. Very distressed, he went and shouted over the wall, 'Mr Hine, Mr Earl, war has broken out.' They never lifted their heads up, just went on throwing their quoits, and said 'Oh aye?' That was how the news of the First World War was received. I can remember a shortage of food at the beginning of the war. You weren't hungry but you couldn't get bread, and my mother made her own bread which was lovely.

When I was five, I went to a dame's school that was run by two unmarried ladies, both called Miss Hargreaves. They had taken an empty house at the bottom of Gillinggate and turned it into a school. There was very few books and we learnt from a large poster on the wall. The teacher went along with a pointer to each word on the poster and we each read out a sentence in turn. I was bored stiff, as my father had taught me to read when I was three and a half. We were given a writing book, and across the top of the page, in copperplate, there was a proverb – like, 'All that glitters is not gold' – which we wrote out twelve times. Then, if we were lucky, with the whole thing splattered with ink and tears, we were allowed to turn over to another proverb and do the same again.

Actually we were very well taught indeed. We were taught geography, again with the pointer and a big map on the wall. We learned all the names of the countries, capital cities and the rivers that ran through the cities. Of course there was arithmetic and it was 'two ones are two', all through to the twelves. I don't remember anyone being naughty or stepping out of line. No, there was no need for discipline. I think the teachers must have been quite advanced because we had milk every lunchtime.

From the age of four I was taken to church every Sunday morning. I'd be about six years old when I was taken to Sunday School and also to the Sunday evening services. Everybody went to church – it was a sign of respectability. The Zion Chapel was a huge church and inside it had a gallery all the way round. At nights the gallery was packed with young people, and you couldn't have got a seat. It was the same on the ground floor, which was packed with older people. At home we'd say grace before meals. We'd bow our heads and my father would say grace, then we could all fall to and eat. It was a very normal household really.

I led my own life, playing with the little girl along the street, in each other's houses and playing with our dolls. We played in the woods and all over the place. You see, it was quite safe. Nothing ever happened to anybody. And I was so young. In those days when you were about seven or eight you were just like a child of three or four is now – completely unsophisticated. We used to leave our dolls' prams in the middle of the road because there was very little traffic. Mrs Tognarelli used to come round in a little pony and cart selling ice-cream every afternoon. She spoke no English at all, except she could say 'Ta' when you gave her your penny.

The quarries were working then, of course. The huge stones were brought by cart, down past our house, down across Windermere Road and up the side of Kendal Green. At the top of the Green sat a group of paupers from the poorhouse, breaking stones. They sat there all day,

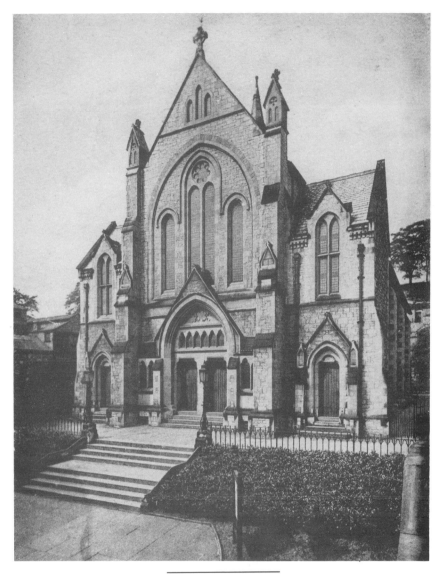

Zion Chapel, Kendal

winter and summer. When it rained they covered themselves up with sacks. When I was with my mother on her church visits, she always spoke to these men as we passed. She used to say to me, 'Now speak to these men', and she'd say 'Good afternoon' but never got an answer. My father was on the Board of Guardians for the poorhouse. However he never spoke about it at home.

Zion Chapel outing on Grasmere, c. 1910

When I went with my mother on her church visits, we walked. As we didn't have a pony and trap, we were considered very poor. We'd visit church members and I'd be lifted on to a chair and sat with my poor little legs dangling and never speak unless I was spoken to. 'And how are you, Rita?' would say a lady and I'd whisper, 'Very well, thank you.'

We always had a maid. She'd be paid five shillings a week. Assisted by my mother, the maid did all the work. Then, in the afternoon, dressed up in a black dress and a little white cap on her head, she would answer the door when the callers came. Every three weeks my mother had an 'at home' when all the ladies of the congregation came. The visitors all had a silver visiting card case, and when they were leaving they left calling cards.

We had three maids at different times. One was Elizabeth Morland, she came off the slums on Fellside. Another girl was from Newcastle, I don't remember her very well. Then we had Janet Frosso, who was a Greek. She tipped my pram up and bruised me badly, then bundled me back saying, 'Don't tell anybody.' When my mother was bathing me, she saw those awful bruises and Janet Frosso disappeared. Buried in the garden perhaps! I don't know.

When I was going to town with my mother we used to go past Fellside which had a dreadful reputation. If you came off Fellside you were damned immediately. I remember the smell. All the pipes were broken

Kendal Green, near the poorhouse

and I don't think there was any loos because people just came out and relieved themselves in the road. My mother would say, 'Don't look, this little boy is going to be very rude.' And we hurried by with averted eyes, while the little boy had a pee.

My father worked endlessly for the poor who lived in the yards off Highgate. They had terrible houses, just hovels, and so dark. From nearly every house there was someone with tuberculosis, and eventually they'd go to Meathop Sanatorium and die there.

I don't remember much about the children from Fellside or Highgate because I wouldn't be allowed to play with them. The only time I ever came across them was in Sunday School if we put on a play and I was in it. I thought these children were wonderful because they weren't like the children I was allowed to mix with socially. They had guts. The little boys, especially, were lovely.

We had one holiday a year, for a fortnight. We went to Morecambe which, to me, was the high spot. My sister Mildred and my father took their bicycles and went cycling every day. Mother and I sat on the sands. She had her crochet work and I had a spade and made sand pies. Morecambe had a tower where they had variety shows. There'd be a comedian, and a soubrette [dancer], along with other acts and a short film. The first time I saw a film, I was so frightened I got under the seat. The film showed a railway train approaching at high speed, out of the

Fellside, Kendal

screen, as I thought. So I saved myself by getting under the seat. We used to go to pierrot shows which my father was very fond of. These were in the open air and accompanied by an old broken-down piano.

In June 1919 we moved from Kendal to Lytham St Anne's. The congregation pleaded with my father to stay – he was very popular. No, that's the wrong word. He was respected. We travelled by train from Kendal to Lancashire. Kendal Station was very important in those days. From Queen's Road we used to sit at the window and see the trains toiling up Shap. They were pushed from the back by another little engine. It was very interesting to watch.

Our house in Lytham was surrounded by fields. Lovely, really, but my sister and I hated Lytham and used to say, 'We'll go back to Kendal, we'll go back some day.' I loved Kendal but disliked Lytham for the snobbery. It was a *nouveau riche* place. I was once staying at a town, and when I was leaving I said to someone, 'I've never been to a more unfriendly place.' They answered, 'Well, you never showed your passport.' I asked, 'What passport?' The reply was 'Your bankbook.' Lytham was like that. The congregation was much wealthier than in Kendal. They were nearly all 'cotton people' who owned mills. Later, as a result of the First World War, their shares became absolutely valueless. People who owned two or three mills were brought down to nothing. It was dreadful, as most of them were elderly. I think a lot of them were killed with the shock. Others had to go out to work as shop assistants or clerks.

At first I went to a little private school. As I neared eleven years of age, I had to go to school in Blackpool because there was no secondary one in Lytham then. About this time my mother died. She'd been ill for so long and in such a messy way, as she had cancer of the throat. There was a little tube that she breathed through in her throat, then a tube in her nose, which we fed her through. My mother knew she was dying and wrote a letter to my father, telling him to marry again, for someone to look after us both. He did remarry and it was my mother's sister, so he married his sister-in-law. I didn't get on with her, as we were both what is known as high-spirited.

I loathed school. I hated discipline – I do to this day. Anyone telling me, 'You know Rita, you ought to do this' or 'Why don't you . . .' oh I could get up and scrag them. I've always been like that. The headmistress asked for me to be taken away from school. She sent for my father and said, 'Rita will never get through matriculation', which was rather like 'A' levels. I fought against discipline so much, I didn't learn anything. The only subjects I liked were history and English. I wanted to be a milliner but in those days you were told by your parents what to do.

My sister wanted to be a pianist but she had to be a teacher. So at sixteen I went to a commercial college in Preston. I was there for more than a year learning shorthand, typing, book-keeping and office principles.

During all this time everything my sister and I did had to be connected with the church. Nearly every night of the week we had to go to some kind of church meeting. There was the Ladies Sewing Meeting – oh I can't tell you how ghastly it was. That was on a Monday night. Tuesday night was the Sisterhood, which was even more ghastly. Wednesday night was the Church Meeting, when all the members got together. Thursday night was the Ladies Circle, oh very posh. Friday night was choir practice and Saturday night I had to myself.

The church members were so censorious and they watched you because you were young. They watched you all the time and you just had to make one tiny slip and Dad was told. 'Oh Rita was seen doing so and so' or 'Rita was seen talking to somebody.' It was dreadful, dreadful. My father would storm at me – he had such a temper. He never hit me, it was all done with the tongue. Mother had been a great slapper and I liked her punishments because you got it and that was that. But Dad would go quiet, not speak for two or three days, and that was most cruel.

I escaped by joining the Operatic Society, which was my downfall because I hadn't realised there were people like that in the world. Oh, it was lovely to be away from those awful church people, and that's when I began to go on the downward path. Dad couldn't interfere, as nearly half the Operatic Society were people from other churches. He couldn't remove his daughter from the hands of Satan if she was sitting next to somebody from another church. I don't know what would have happened to me if I hadn't got into that society. We had such fun. We did musical comedies and you'd be surprised to know I often played the comedienne.

After I left college I had trouble getting a job, as there were three million unemployed then. I wrote eighty-seven letters to companies and in the end I didn't get my first job by writing. Dad went to a meeting somewhere and a man asked what I was doing. Dad told him I couldn't get a job and the man said, 'Oh, I'll give her one.' He never asked what I could do or anything and I got a job with the London, Midlands and Scottish Railway, working in the office. It was only temporary while someone was ill, and when they came back to work I got a job in a cotton mill at Preston.

I worked at the mill as a shorthand typist which I hated because I didn't want to do this type of work. About two years later, my stepmother left my father, so I was brought home to run the house and look after him. I was very happy to leave the office. It was like coming out of prison because I never thought I'd be able to leave there. My father was losing his sight very rapidly, so I did everything for him. I ran the house, wrote all his letters, dealt with his correspondence, led him about and acted as hostess at church affairs.

I had some free time but I had to fight for it. I still went to the Operatic Society and we started a Dramatic Society at church with plays, which I produced and acted in. I've always had lots of friends and some weren't connected with the church.

The war didn't make any difference to the sort of life I was living. Just outside Lytham was a big camp with several thousand Yanks. This went down well with the local girls. Oh, the Yanks were a shocking lot, they really were. So brash. What was the saying? 'Overseas, overpaid and oversexed.' And that was very true of them, as they were very troublesome.

My sister, who was now married, went back to teaching at a local school and I looked after her young son. So, besides my blind father, I also had a two-year-old child. I'd looked after Dad for about fifteen years when he died in 1943. Then I trained to do welfare work.

In those days there were teachers of the blind and you worked for a local authority. They don't do that now, welfare people do everything. I trained at the Royal School for the Blind in Birmingham. My training should have been for two years but, as I'd been a clergyman's daughter and used to visiting, it was cut down to eighteen months. Then I got my own patch at Willesden in London.

I enjoyed the work very much. I visited all the blind people who were living with relatives, to check that they were being looked after. If they wished I'd teach them braille, knitting or cooking. My greatest difficulty was with authority. They didn't like people to use their initiative. You were supposed to go and ask at the office, 'Please may I go and do such and such a thing.' I was very apt to go and do it, then tell them, and I got into a lot of trouble. The conditions for blind people at that time were quite good really. I didn't come across anybody in dire straits, we looked after them you see. When the bombing got very, very bad, we moved about seventy blind people from my area into the country. They went to a lovely mansion, a beautiful place.

I returned to Lytham to sell Dad's house and, when I was doing this, the war ended. I never returned to London, as I took a job as a trainee pub-keeper at the Punch Bowl in Crosthwaite. I'd always fancied a pub and I worked at the bar downstairs. The Captain, who ran the pub, had the bar upstairs with all the hoi polloi but I had the country lads. The lads were grand, once they'd stopped pulling my leg and cheating me. As soon as they found out I was born in Kendal I was all right.

While I was working at the Punch Bowl some people came to stay who had a lovely house at Grange-Over-Sands. They asked me to go and be their housekeeper, so I went there for eighteen months. The lady of the house was lovely but her nurse companion wasn't. I returned to Lytham, where my sister and I took a shop. We sold knitting wool and picture prints. It was a terrible worry financially, as we hadn't enough capital.

We ran the shop for about ten years and then I went blind. Of course I had to come out of the shop then. My sight went gradually at the beginning and very quickly at the end. I wasn't bitter. It was just a feeling, 'Well, this is it.' Because, you see, it was hereditary and there was no escape. I had three operations but they didn't do any good.

My sister Mildred and her husband were much older than I was. So, when it came to retiring time, the shop was sold and that was when we came here. Mildred and I had always said we'd go back to Kendal when we retired and I've been very happy here, though my sister and her husband have since died.

I realised very early after I went blind that, if I didn't try to keep up intellectually, I was going to become a sort of 'nothing'. I've always listened to the radio and the people who come to see me, luckily they've all got brains. They talk to me and keep me up to date, which pleases me greatly. Very often they mention something and I'll say, 'Oh yes, I know about that.' It makes me very happy that I'm still mentally alert.

I have no religion – I read myself out of it. I believe that Jesus Christ was a wonderful man, like Mohammed and other great teachers and saints, but I've got no religion. It's nothing to do with my blindness, the religion had gone long before that came. I told my father I'd lost my faith. He said, 'Well I can't do anything for you. You're going through a very dark wood and when you come out into the sunshine on the other side you'll find you've brought your faith with you.' And I have brought my faith but it wasn't his faith. It was the faith I have now in goodness and kindness and love. I think, when you die, that's the end. I hope it is. I wouldn't want to go on because you wouldn't know if it was going to be better or worse, would you?

EIGHT

'I learnt to milk cows when I was seven'

MARY HAYHURST (b. 1918)
Ravenstonedale/Kings Meaburn

My mother was born at Ravenstonedale and later went into service for the local gentry. There was a lot of gentry in the area in those days – they were the landowners with beautiful big houses. Mother worked for a Lady Fletcher and her sister, then some people called Fothergill who were well off. Dad was a farmworker from Greenholme but used to work on farms at Crook and Staveley, down that way. When my parents married they lived at Coldbeck, which was a part of Ravenstonedale. The other part was called Gallows Hill where they used to have hangings.

I was born at Coldbeck in 1918. Our house had a living-room, two **bedrooms and a scullery-cum-pantry. For lighting, we just had an old**

Coldbeck, Ravenstonedale (Mary was born in the end house on the left)

83

Mary as a toddler

paraffin lamp and candles but later on we got an Aladdin lamp. The toilet was outside, and we shared it with the house next door. It was the schoolhouse and the master, Mr Butt, lived there with his daughter. Later, when they left, the next Head, Tommy Raines, moved in. My grandmother lived with us and she was a lovely old lady. Tall and very thin, she always wore a long black skirt and white apron. Grandma was once standing in the doorway with me in her arms as a baby, when a thunderbolt dropped. The bolt blew the sink out of the pantry and the garden tiles off. It also burnt all the ivy off the house and sent Grandma stone deaf.

Some of the gentry and the local vicar asked Mother if she would take in their washing – you might say she was a laundress. It was very hard work for her because she had to go and collect their washing and bring it home. It was all to wash, boil, blue and starch. Everything was to iron and then carry back to the big houses. I can remember Mother had a

Mary's grandmother and mother

great big black pan to boil her whites that she used to hang over the fire on the old-fashioned range. She also had a little jiffy washer with an agitator inside, not electric of course. Before that she would just have a tub and stir the washing with a posser. We had a long back yard with a clothes line, where Mother dried the clothes. And when the weather was bad there was a full clothes maiden round the fire.

I was five years old when I started Ravenstonedale School and I was there all my school years. It wasn't very far away, just through the churchyard and the orchard. Inside the school was a great big room divided into two, and a smaller classroom. We had a nice big old stove, and if it was snowy weather, and you needed to change your footwear or anything, it was always hung to dry on the guard round the stove. They didn't like us to wear Wellingtons for school, so we went in clogs. The toilets were outside but don't mention them – they were horrible. We had a headmaster, two teachers and usually two pupil teachers. School

Ravenstonedale School, c. 1929 (Mary is second row from the back, centre)

was all right but discipline was strict. The first headmaster, Mr Raines, was a bit bad-tempered really. When he left, the next headmaster, Mr Walker, used to have a big strap. I never ever got the strap – I managed to get out of that.

I'm left-handed but at school they made me write with my right, so now I can use both. The only thing was, when we did dress-making, I was made to cut out the material with my right hand and spoilt it all. So that was it. I never did any more, and I can cut ever so well with my left hand.

Just after I started school Grandma died and, shortly after, my dad took a farm between Ravenstonedale and Newbiggin-on-Lune. This meant that I had about a mile and a half to walk to school every day but I didn't take sandwiches with me like other children. An aunt and uncle, who had no children of their own and lived quite near the school, insisted I had to go to their house for my dinner. Our farm was about twenty acres and we had cows, sheep, pigs, hens, geese – a bit of everything really. The house had four big bedrooms, a boxroom, kitchen, sitting-rooms, and two big dairies.

My dad didn't have anybody to help him on the farm, just my mother and me. I learnt to milk cows when I was seven. At first we made butter and cheese, until Express Dairies started up. The milk was separated and with the cream we made butter and great big cheeses. For our Wensleydale cheese we put rennet into the milk to make it curdle. You used to work it all up, put it into these big vats, then into a cheese press. When they were dry enough, they were put on to shelves in one of the bedrooms to dry out. Parkin's, who were the big grocers at Appleby, used to come and see the cheese was all right and buy it off us. The calves were fed on the milk and the pigs' feed was mixed with the whey from the cheese and the separated milk.

I was an only child but there was plenty of children to play with. I had cousins and friends who lived nearby, it was grand. Then a friend lived over the road and we played football with the lads and cricket when the season came in. We used to go to Kirkby Stephen now and again but our main days were the Band of Hope Demonstration Days, the annual day trip to Morecambe with them, and the Sunday School trip.

We'd moved to the farm in 1924 and by 1927 it was terrible with the Depression. My dad had to go out to work to keep things going. He went and worked on other farms, then worked for the council for a while. With his horse and cart he moved rubbish and stones for the council, when they were tarring the roads. Dad used to do any jobs that were going, just to keep his head above water. They really were hard times.

On Christmas Eve I'd go with my mam and dad to visit some friends, and on New Year's Eve they'd return our visit. Being an only child and having so many aunts and uncles, they all used to give me presents at Christmas. I'd be given a doll and all kinds of things that would go into my pillowcase. On Christmas Day there was only the three of us at dinnertime. We usually had a goose because we had our own geese. We bred them to sell for Christmas, them and chickens, and had them all to pluck and do. On Christmas Day we went to church, and as I was in the church choir we used to go singing before Christmas. We went round the village singing and to the big houses. We didn't go into the houses, as we had to get round all the village. It was lovely, lovely in those days. I liked the olden days better because there was no television and you had such a grand social life among your friends and relations.

I used to go to Sunday School and at Easter we always used to go to church with pasche eggs and oranges in a decorated basket. These were taken up to the altar and then taken to Kendal Hospital. The pasche eggs had been boiled in onion peelings and we'd keep some back to roll down the hills. We always used to be dressed up for Easter Sunday – a lovely new bonnet, new dress, ankle socks and sandals. It's never good weather now. We haven't been able to get dressed up for Easter in our thin clothes for a few years now.

There was a lot going on in the villages, as the big houses had maids and gardeners. Then the farmers often had maids and hired men as well. The gentry used to take part in the village life but in those days there was that real class distinction. The poor often had six or eight in a family. The gentry were the gentry and we were the poor. Then they would have three or four maids – well now they can't afford it. But they were good people, they were nice. Now everybody is down to more or less the same, aren't they? Of course there was no holiday homes, just two hotels at Ravenstonedale that took in visitors. There weren't many tourists but quite a few walkers and these were more of the well-off people that did come. Ordinary folk didn't get away much.

Mind you, I was lucky. We had six weeks' summer holiday from school and I used to have a month's holiday with an aunt and uncle who lived in Bradford. After my month with them, I'd go to Darlington and stay with another aunt and uncle who also had no family. My uncle at Darlington was a joiner, a cabinet-maker, and he worked for the School Furnishing Company. And at school at Ravenstonedale all the desks had the name of that company on them. Uncle used to help to make those desks.

I left school the week after I was fourteen. Most children left at that age unless they 'passed' and went to the grammar school. I wanted to be a hairdresser but my parents didn't want me to. I just had to stay at home and help with the farm. I didn't get a wage, I got all my clothes bought for me and was given pocket money. I just had to ask and I got what I wanted but there was no wages.

At home I helped milk the cows and worked in the house. I used to scrub all the floors and there were no carpets then, just mats. Then I'd do the bedrooms and eventually I did the baking. Haytime and sheep-clipping time were the busiest times, but really it was busy all year round. You see, all the work was done by hand. Mind, the weather was better than it is now for working in the hayfields. You could go and get a field ready and leave it until the next day. You knew it was going to be fine weather, whereas now you can't do that.

By 1936 we had electricity. All these pylons were put in, through our fields. It did make a difference but you were only allowed one plug in each room in those days. Shortly after this we moved to another farm, which was on the main Ravenstonedale to Kendal road. This farm was bigger but the house wasn't as large as the one we'd had.

We had quite a lot of tramps calling at the farm because of the workhouse at Kirkby Stephen. They were let out of the workhouse at about eight o'clock in the morning and by nine o'clock they'd be coming through on their way to Kendal, begging for food at the door. There were loads of tramps – some were all right and some you'd be scared of. They were mostly elderly men on their way to the workhouse at Kendal to get fed and put up but they'd be begging on the roads in between.

These men used to put secret signs on the walls to tell the next ones where they could get something to eat. You could guarantee, you'd have three or four of them at once. Not every day but now and again. Very rarely you'd see a woman with them.

The chap who had lived on the farm before us had a small milk round and I took it over. Oh, it was hard work. It was only a walking round, carrying all these heavy cans of milk, but in frosty weather you could hardly stand sometimes. The winters were really bad with frost and snow. I had the job of taking milk to the school at Ravenstonedale and when the war started there was quite a lot of evacuees. So Dad made me a bogie [small wooden cart] to put the milk on, as it was too heavy to carry. The milk for the school was put into one-third pint bottles every day but the rest was put into a big can. I used to measure the milk out into jugs for the houses.

In Ravenstonedale there was lots going on in those days. We went to dances, socials and whist drives. People went backwards and forwards to folk's houses. You had more of a social life in the village with your friends and we had a few relatives we went to see at nights. There wasn't the cars on the roads then but it didn't bother me walking home alone in the dark.

My mother had always liked music and she bought me a piano. My auntie got it for us at Bradford and I went for music lessons to Kirkby Stephen every Saturday. I sat exams and passed them but I was never that interested, as all I'd wanted to do was be a hairdresser. For a while I gave music lessons at home and charged fifteen shillings a quarter. I was a bit shy to go out socialising and play the piano but I did like playing the church organ. I loved that.

A chap who used to play the organ taught me how to play and I had to have somebody to blow the bellows for me. The young lads didn't enjoy doing this and I used to give them so much a week for doing it. Ravenstonedale church is very, very old and has three pulpits. The middle pulpit was used, and when it was time to read the lesson the Bible was on this beautiful brass eagle. And some of the seats, instead of facing the altar were facing the other way.

You walked right up the aisle, and when you were there, you were sitting looking at the congregation. The gentry had their own seats, which were more or less at the front. You know when you say the Creed? Well, it was on the wall behind us and everybody had to turn round in their seats to read it. At that time, the church had oil lamps – I do remember that and the gallery and the beautiful organ. It was really well attended was the church. I played there morning and evening on a Sunday and used to teach there as well. When I had to teach, I had to go up them steps into one of the pulpits. It's a beautiful church and well worth going to see.

When the war started I wanted to be in the WRAF and be a driver. I'd always wanted to drive – that was my one ambition. We had two travellers come round to the farm and one day when I was talking to them I said, 'If I've to go in the WRAF I want to learn to drive.' So one of the travellers said, 'I'll take you and teach you to drive.' I had two lessons with him and he left me in a field on my own, just driving round and changing gear. Oh, it was great. I had those two lessons and then I was off, as there was no test to pass in those days. Dad got me off going into the forces because he hadn't anybody helping him except me, so that was it. But I really did want to join up.

When the war started we had an evacuee from Barrow-in-Furness come to live with us and he settled in really well. At the end of the war Dad wanted him to stay, as he had really loved living on the farm. A lot of the evacuees enjoyed their stay in the country. The house opposite us was taken over by a big private school and these four maids came with them. They were lovely girls and I got on well with them. I remember one lovely moonlit night when we all walked to Kirkby Stephen. You couldn't see the wall tops for the snow but it was beautiful. Another time, I'd gone to the pictures at Kirkby Stephen and met a friend there. When we came out it had started snowing and I couldn't get back home. I had to walk to Nateby, a nearby village, to my godmother's. It was midnight when I reached her house and knocked her up. Icicles were hanging off my hair – frozen I was. The weather was that bad I had to stay there four or five days until the school bus got through and I could get a lift into town.

In 1942 Dad had to get out of the farm. The landlord wanted the farm for himself, so we just had to find another place. A cousin of my father's, who was retiring from a farm at King's Meaburn, asked Dad if he wanted to take it over and we came here. I came by cattle wagon and it was thick snow then as well. Coming over the moors, an army convoy had to pull in to let us through as there was only one track. It was terrible snow. We didn't know anybody here at all when we came, as Dad's cousin had left. But my aunt and uncle from Bradford came to live with us about that time, as Auntie was bad with her nerves and had heart trouble. They came away from the bombing because she couldn't stand it any longer. They were in their sixties and super people so we all got on very well together.

Just before we came here, Dad bought a little old Morris 8 and it was always breaking down. We had many a laugh about that car. When we moved here, one night we were going over to Ravenstonedale in it. There was Dad, our evacuee, a farm lad, and me who was driving. We were going over to Orton when there was this almighty bang. Both the tube and tyre had blown, so we had to turn round and come back on just the bare rim. Another night, coming home, just past the church at Orton the horn started to blow. None of us knew how to stop it, so it blew all the way home. Oh, I could write a book about that car.

When we moved to Kings Meaburn rents were paid at a different time. Back at Ravenstonedale everybody paid their rents on 12th May, and if they were moving that was the day they left their farm. At King's Meaburn, moving day was Candlemas, 2nd February.

During the war we had to plough and produce everything – potatoes, oats, barley, everything. One year the weather was terrible. We never did finish getting the crops in, it was so wet. It's very clay-like, the soil round here, and it holds water.

I'd seen my future husband going backwards and forwards past our farm with his horse and cart. My auntie said, 'Oh, there's a real nice young man', but I wasn't interested, as I was going with somebody else at the time. Then one day he came and asked Dad if I could help him with sowing his corn. You see, in those days you 'threw' the corn and had to have somebody to fill the bag up. Anyway Dad said, 'Mary will come and help you.' So I had to go and help and he got me talked round to going out with him.

I was twenty-five when I got married and didn't have a proper wedding dress – just a blue two-piece – with the war being on. We all had to pool our coupons to get the wedding cake made. There was no honeymoon, as my husband couldn't get anyone to do his work for him. He lived on a farm with his mother and sister, but when we married they moved into the cottage next door. I've lived here for fifty-two years now and always had neighbours in my yard so I must be easy to get on with.

I still worked in the fields when I was married, even after my children were born. I used to go out at haytime and help my husband whenever it was necessary. My husband had always been in farming and when he was young he went to work on other farms. He said some of the places were terrible. You had to sit on your own to have your meals, and at one place he wasn't even allowed to sleep in the actual house. He didn't stay long there. Yet some places he went to, they were really good. When we had hired lads they always ate with us. I think we spoilt them, they never wanted to leave.

My children were all born at home. A nurse used to come and visit me quite often to see that I was all right. Then, when the baby was due, she'd come and send for the doctor if it was necessary. If it wasn't, she delivered the baby herself. After my first was born I was in bed a fortnight. It was terrible – they wouldn't let me get up. They did that in those days, they kept you in bed. Mind, I had bad legs (likely with working a lot) but the doctor used to come and see how I was. The doctor had to visit people because they hadn't cars in those days to go to him.

When I was laid up, a local lady would come to look after the family and house, and cook meals for my husband and the lad. There used to be ladies that did that job in those days. You booked her to come and help and she'd pop in and help me before the baby was born. Then she'd be there to help the nurse and she'd stay on for maybe a fortnight. When my two youngest children were born I had a friend in the village who came and helped me, which was grand. By that time I wasn't in bed very long. The newer nurses got you up earlier.

A lot of us used to hire a car and go to dances all over the place. My husband didn't like dancing, so I went with two of my friends. We also had some good concerts in the village. I remember one chap who was a marvellous yodeller. He used to say it soothed the cows.

One of the concert parties at Kings Meaburn Village Hall, c. 1960
Fred Lowis, 'the yodeller', is at the back (fifth from the left) and Mary's daughter
Ann is at the front (third from the right)

Kings Meaburn has changed since we came here. Vans used to come round every day – we didn't need to go shopping really. In the village was a joiner's shop, petrol pumps, a blacksmith's, shoemaker's, the pub, post office and general store. Now there's only the pub, shop and post office all in one. The local school has closed, as there wasn't enough pupils. The children go to Crosby Ravensworth until they're eleven and then the bus takes them to Appleby Secondary school. And farms . . . there's only three farms left and there used to be quite a few small-holdings. Of course farming has changed, it's all mechanised now. It's different altogether – with all these forms to fill in. And it's getting worse, I hear, with these EEC rules. There's a lot of strangers, as houses that have come up for sale have been bought as holiday homes. So the village has altered an awful lot.

A caravan park opened down the road and a general shop was needed, as the lady who kept the last one had died. So I started a shop in this front room. I started up in about 1970 and had it here for about three years. I sold most things, and if I didn't have what a customer wanted I'd get it. Bread was delivered to me but on my half-day, which was Tuesday, I'd go to the wholesaler's at Penrith and buy my stuff in. It was hard work but everybody would be coming in and having a natter. I did enjoy it.

I gave the shop up when I couldn't get any help and then I went out to work. First I went to work in Penrith at a café. Then when it closed down I went to another café at Appleby. That packed in, so I worked part-time at a wallpaper shop and at nights worked as a barmaid in two pubs. After that I helped a friend of ours who went into business and I've helped out part-time ever since. Then I've got my newspapers – that's why everybody keeps coming in. All the newspapers are delivered here in big bundles between seven and eight o'clock in the morning. I've them all to sort out and the locals start coming for them about half-past eight. On a Saturday morning, people come for their *Cumberland and Westmorland Herald* and pay me.

A neighbour's daughter from across the way worked at a school and they asked, 'Did she know anybody who'd take the time to talk to the children?' so she gave my name. About three times a year I have kiddies come from a school to ask me questions about the olden days and I tell them what I can. I've always been busy, I can't bear not to be. I mean if you'd not been here, I'd have been doing something.

I still drive and go to Bolton Mother's Union and the Women's Institute there, which is only a few miles away. I play indoor bowls and dominoes every week. Then there's a place at High Hesket on the way to Carlisle that I go to when there's Country and Western music on. Once I wanted to live down at Kendal. Then I looked out of this window and thought, 'Oh what a lovely view, I don't want to leave it.' Although we get all the wild weather, all the winds and everything, when it's fine it's beautiful. From this room you look across on to the Lakeland hills and I can go to the back window and see all the Pennines. I wouldn't like to live anywhere else.

NINE

'You hadn't to waste a minute'

DOLLY (b. 1908)
Kentmere/Windermere/Staveley

'This is the lassie that was born with the wee lambies.' I felt awful at school when old Dr Henderson used to say that. You see, my mother used to take in visitors at Kentmere and the school doctor was staying at Easter 1908. My Aunt Sarah had to get him out of bed when my mother went into labour and he brought me into the world.

My father was a quarryman at Kentmere quarry, and when he married my mother they set up home at Kentmere. Mother had eight children, of which I was the youngest, but three died when they were small. My father's mother lived with us and she'd been the Kentmere postwoman for twenty-one years. It was estimated that in her time she had walked one and a third times round the world. Grandma always said she'd carried more pieces of plough and packets of yeast to the farms than she had letters.

We lived at Raw Cottage. Now it's spelt 'RAWE' and been altered but it's been kept as near as possible to what it was like when we were children. The house had just one door and a little porch where we did our laundry and washing up. Once or twice a day, water had to be carried in buckets from the stream down the field and set on a big stone slab in the porch. Inside was quite a nice, large sitting-room with two windows and a spice cupboard. There was a good-sized pantry where Mother kept her baking and things like that. In what we called the parlour Mother had two double beds and a chest of drawers, as she took lodgers in at that time. We had two bedrooms, and the larger one was partitioned off with heavy quilts and curtains. My sister and I slept in one half and my parents in the other.

We had quite a lot of lodgers, usually three or four at a time. They were nearly all quarrymen. All the quarries in the area were working then – it was a proper industry and Kentmere was in full swing. I can remember slate being brought down on flat lorries to Staveley Station.

I was five years old when I started Kentmere School. It was very near where we lived but it's been done away with now. Some children had to walk about three miles to school and the same distance home. There was

Top: Dolly with her grandmother at Rawe Cottage, c. 1912
Above: Dolly at Rawe Cottage almost 60 years later

*Dolly celebrating Empire Day, 24th May,
at Kentmere School, 1913–14*

just one classroom, with a big porch where we hung our coats. The boys'
toilet was outside, down the road, and the girls' was in the back yard
along with the stick shed and coal house. Most of us wore clogs but we
had to take them off in the classroom and put slippers on because of the
noise. Imagine a wooden floor and a heap of children with clogs!

Mrs Voss was our teacher then. Later on we got a pupil teacher
called Miss Dobson. We all used slates and a slate pencil but we didn't do
spellings from a book. All the children stood in a row and we each had to
spell something, then Mrs Voss would give us dictation. The discipline
was very good. You never questioned the teacher. At Christmastime we
always did a little play of some sort and made our own costumes. The
only play I can remember much about was *Humpty Dumpty* and,
needless to say, I was Humpty. If the little ones didn't behave Mrs Voss
made a big dunce's cap and they stood in the corner with the cap on.
When we were older, it was the cane if we didn't behave. We were also
taught sewing, knitting and needlework – things you had to do at home.

The church was next door to the school and St Cuthbert's is
beautiful, with quite a history. Church played a large part in our lives.
On a Sunday we went to morning service, Sunday School and then
afternoon service. We had to go. Father insisted, though he never went
himself. I only ever knew him to go to funerals and weddings. People
used to walk from the top end of Longsleddale over to Kentmere Church

in summer because it was almost as near as their church. Oh, there used to be thirty to forty people on a Sunday afternoon at church. Everyone was involved. At Easter and Harvest Festival they provided flowers and it was a marvellous show.

We had a grand old sexton to look after the oil lamps and there was always somebody to clean the church. The men kept the roses cut and the graves nice. Mrs Voss, the teacher, played the church organ. She had a pony and trap, as most of the better-class people had. While she was at church one Sunday evening some boys from the village took the pony for a ride. When she came back home, there was a knock on her door. 'Please, Mrs Voss, we've found your pony', and she gave them sixpence each for bringing it back. We had many a laugh about that – they'd been riding the blessed thing themselves!

I remember the start of the First World War perfectly well. We were helping in the hayfield belonging to Mr Hayton when we saw a rocket go up. 'That's the war, the war's started,' somebody said. But it didn't register in our minds how serious it really was. At the end of the war I remember the men coming home – and those who didn't – but I was still at an age when it didn't mean much.

At home we used to play cards and dominoes but we were never allowed to play on Sunday. Never. Up until we were quite big, we always stood for meals, as Father would never let us sit at the table. Even when we were older we weren't allowed to sit at the table with visitors – we had to wait until they were gone. And you didn't interrupt. If you did you were in bed before you knew it. That was the old-fashioned way.

When my mother got up in the morning, she had her fire to make, then the lodgers' breakfasts to see to. For this she had a great big frying pan that hung in the grate. After the breakfasts, all the lodgers' packed lunches were put into boxes, as well as ours for school. Little cans with lids on were filled with cold tea for us, then Mother started on her housework. For washing day, she had an old-fashioned copper that was kept in a building outside. This had to be lit and the water boiling before she could start. Of course, all the clothes were to iron and it was done with an old-fashioned flat iron or charcoal one. Then there was the cleaning and the children to look after.

Mother had one day when she baked for the whole week – brown bread, white bread, teacakes and all her own pastry and pies. So you can imagine how much she used to bake, with all the men and children. All this was done in a fireside oven. We had a herb garden, with rosemary, thyme, sage, marjoram and mint. These were gathered and hung up to dry in the living-room. You couldn't do anything with them until they were dry and they were then used for seasoning food. Easterledge –

that's a plant which grows around Easter and its leaves were gathered to make a lovely savoury easterledge pudding.

We also kept poultry and a pig. When the pig was killed, Mother made her own black puddings, sausage and brawn. The pig was slaughtered, and the intestines cleaned and put into salty water before being used to make sausages. The sausage was made with any spare bits of meat, bread and seasoning. The blood of the pig was for making black puddings; then barley, breadcrumbs, different seasonings and so much fat was added. They're no good without the fat. Spare ribs were for roasting but the hams and flitches were cut up and salted. You usually had a stone slab in the pantry where the meat was laid and rubbed with salt to make it sweat. A few weeks later, the meat was taken out of the salt, washed and hung up to dry. Oh, it was a big day killing a pig. Everybody was busy.

In those days you had to pay for the doctor, so home cures were used. One that was used a lot was goose grease for a bad chest. When farmers' wives killed a goose they kept the grease and it was rubbed into the chest. It did smell but people weren't so fussy then. Red flannel was worn a lot by old ladies, as this was good for a bad back or chest. If you had a bad cold, or came in wet from the rain, you put your feet into a mustard bath. And I can see the point of that because very often your feet are the coldest part. Olive oil was used for a bad throat and blackcurrant jam stirred into hot water was a soothing drink.

Living in the country, people bought their flour in five-stone bags, or ten-stone ones for the big houses. When the bags were empty we used to unpick them, and on washing day they'd be put in the boiler with some soda and bleached. From a five-stone bag, we could make two lovely tea towels or a pillowcase. If we had feathers, we could make two cushions. It was surprising what people could make out of these flour bags but we had to do it – there wasn't the money to buy them. We all had to sew, do a bit of embroidery, make rugs, quilting and work like that. It was night work for winter because people didn't go out much. In summer yes, but not winter.

After a rock fall at Kentmere quarry my father went back to being a shepherd at Kentmere Hall. He used to take sheep from Kentmere to Mardale and I often used to go with him. We would walk over Nan Bield Pass, right across to Riggindale, Field Head and over the stile, down to Chapel Hill. At Chapel Hill, Dad used to leave me and go to the pub for a pint. Mother used to encourage me to go to Mardale because, if he went on his own, many a time he'd never come back until the next day.

Mardale was a real country district and it revolved round its church. The people there were told in 1919 that the village was going to be flooded but they didn't believe it. You know what people are like – 'Oh no, they'll never do it' – but of course they did. Well, if people had opposed it, the flooding would never have happened. All the local people had to move out in the 1930s, the farms were sold and the bodies were moved from the churchyard. Mardale was flooded [in 1937] and that was that.

At the time my father worked at Kentmere Hall it belonged to the Wilsons of Rigmaden, near Kirkby Lonsdale. Oh, it was a grand place and a centre for the village. Mr Wilson had a housekeeper, farm workers and a maid, and Dad was the shepherd and did anything else in between. As children we used to go up the old staircase to the top of the pele tower and get our heads in our hands [get told off] because it wasn't safe. In the dairy all the milk was poured into old-fashioned leads. When you went to empty each lead, you put a pail underneath and very slowly let the peg out and the skimmed milk ran into the pail. The leads stood on what we called binks which were stone slabs, the length of the room. You could stand six or seven leads on a bink.

When sheep were being sheared at Kentmere Hall, all the local farmers helped, sitting on creels and shearing by hand. That was a day. There'd be men clipping the sheep, others catching them, some marking the sheep and others taking them away. At evening time, when all the men had finished, they'd have a real slap-up hot meal before going home. A couple of hours later everyone would come back to have a dance and it would go on until early morning. Somebody would play a fiddle and others would do Westmorland clog dancing. That's how I learnt to clog dance – I was taught by the older people who took an interest in younger ones in those days. The elderly men especially, it didn't matter if you were with the Queen, it would be just the same to them. They treated young people as part of the community, which they were. You had to mind your manners but if they met you going down into the village, it was 'Hello m'lass, where you going?' They never passed without speaking.

My mother used to come into Staveley about every three weeks to do her shopping. There was so many industries then. Staveley had five or six bobbin mills, and at Barley Bridge old Mr Robinson had a corn mill. The village was full of life and everybody worked but still had time for each other. I had been named after a relation who owned the Eagle and Child pub at Staveley and when I was older I used to help with the cleaning there. On wash day all the outside sinks, windowsills and wash house had to be cleaned. It was a busy hotel, with posh folks going into the parlour for a cup of tea. The everyday drinks were beer and stout, there were no fancy drinks at all. You never saw a woman in a pub unless she came to buy a jug of beer to take home.

However we didn't need to go into Staveley much, as grocer's carts came round the district to get your order, which they delivered the week after. Then there was a man who came selling hardware, clothes pegs and all the little things you needed. He also sold paraffin because it was all paraffin lamps in those days. Otherwise farmers and anyone who had a horse and trap used to go to Kendal Market on a Saturday. It was a wonderful old market at Kendal, it really was. In the Market Hall, down each side and in the middle, farmers' wives had their pitches. They sold butter, eggs, fowl, vegetables and fruit. In the Market Place and down New Road were the outdoor markets. The Shambles had some lovely shops, including the Penny Bazaar. The Bazaar sold all the household items you might need, and very few of them cost more than sixpence.

To reach Kendal my mother and me had to walk from Kentmere to Staveley Station, then catch the train to Kendal. The hirings were held in Kendal Market Place where the war memorial is, at Brunskill's corner. These were held on 11th November, at Martinmas, and a farmer and hired man would shake on a deal with one shilling. What would the men get? Between £6 and £8 for six months.

I've often thought down the years what an awfully hard life it must have been for my mother. She never really had any help at all. One of my sisters lived at home for a long time but she went to work in other people's houses. As well as her housework, Mother cleaned the school and church, took in washing and did baking for Kentmere Hall. When their hunting season was over, the hounds were fostered out and she always took a few hounds. My mother also looked after a holiday home, cleaning it and doing baking for the residents. She did all this for a little bit extra because wages weren't anything. Mother hadn't been well for a long time but died very suddenly when she was forty-nine.

I was nearly fifteen when Mother died and was going to stay on at school to be a pupil teacher. That had been my mother's wish but Dad didn't want me to stay on or be a teacher. 'You'll go out and earn your living,' he said. Dad was the old-fashioned sort. He didn't want me for anything else but to work, be a servant. Oh, he was a very good father but quick-tempered. Some parents were really too bad. I only remember him hitting me once – and I asked for it. But, you see, Dad started work when he was eleven – farm work and then the quarries. So, of course, I went into service.

I went to a place at Windermere as a general maid. The couple I worked for were from away and had previously run a hotel. Now they had a big house and only took in guests who were – what shall I say? – better class. I had to learn everything there. My employers were good but extremely old-fashioned and everything had to be just so.

Dolly, 1925

My wage was five shillings a week and I had one half-day off a week and one full day a month. On my day off I had to be back by ten at night, to clear away the evening meal. As I was the only staff, a lady came at first to help with the baking but gradually I got to doing it all. The only other time we had help was with spring-cleaning. In summer I started work at quarter to five in the morning, and when we had visitors it was often midnight when I went to bed. As business was quiet in the winter, I started work at quarter to eight in the mornings.

First thing in the morning, when I got up, I had to clean the living-room and dining-room grates and light the fires. If we had visitors, I'd scrub the front-door steps and clean the brasses. Those were my first jobs, before laying the tables and making breakfasts. After that there was the usual clearing up and cleaning. The proprietors kept poultry and very often the only recreation I got was feeding the hens. I loved doing that because I got half to three-quarters of an hour off in the afternoon to feed them.

When I first started work I found that the lady of the house opened my letters. So I said to Mr Martindale, the postman, 'Please, when you have any letters for me, put them under the doormat, will you?' And that's what he did. You see, the lady was old and thought it was her right to know everything I did. But it wasn't on, that sort of thing. Later on, I used to pop into the village for the evening paper but it was straight there and back. If I was ten minutes late, it was 'Where have you been?'

I very rarely managed to get home because I had to catch the bus to Staveley, then cycle to Kentmere. Besides, everyone at home was working when I had my half-day off. Christmas and Easter were busy times and I had to work. The proprietors would usually give me a diary or a religious book as a Christmas present. I was expected to go to church if we weren't busy, but if I was late back they wanted to know where I'd been and what hymns had been played. Well, the church magazine always had which hymns were to be sung, so I went to my friend's house instead of going to church. With not having a mother, my friend's parents were like parents to me.

Oh, some of the guests were very nice indeed. There was quite a bit of class distinction but I don't think people thought so much about it really. All the hotels and big houses had a full staff. When the maids came off duty at night, it was nothing to see thirty coming from one hotel. Unbelievable! A lot of the hotel work was seasonal and the staff often came back each year, usually from the Newcastle area or Millom.

Like everywhere, there were good and bad employers. I knew of one lady who couldn't keep her staff, as she was a very austere person. One of the gardeners had complained about his food and she said, 'I consider one kipper is good enough for any working man's breakfast, he doesn't need anything else.' The cook at this place was a friend of mine and had been given a basket of gooseberries by someone to make jam with. So, between tea and the evening meal, the cook thought she would top and tail these gooseberries when in walked 'her ladyship'. 'What are you doing, Winifred?' she asked. Winifred told 'her ladyship', who threw all the gooseberries on the fire, saying, 'I don't pay you to do that.' Now that's true. Even though the jam was for the house, it wasn't considered work. You hadn't to waste a minute.

We enjoyed our time off, and if I had a half-day off on a Sunday a group of us local girls would either go walking or down to the lake. For a shilling each we could get a boat and go all round the lake. It was lovely because there wasn't all the motorboats and skiers there is today. Windermere wasn't very big but we could get most things we needed there. I used to go to a little shop (where Thompson and Matthews is now) where you could buy aprons, stockings, elastic, buttons, little caps and all that you wanted. There was hat shops, paper shops, dress shops and they were interesting little places. Yes, Windermere was an elite sort of place but it was lovely – all the big houses with their beautiful gardens.

Bowness used to have a carnival, which was marvellous. The bandstand was open then and the band used to play and people danced on the prom. It was a great day and we were allowed out until half-past eleven at night to watch the fireworks. There was also an agricultural show at Bowness but I didn't win anything when I entered cakes or bread. However Brown and Poulson had a baking competition and I entered a Madeira cake which got first prize of five shillings. Of course I was in the doghouse, being only seventeen and beating a lot of housewives.

I was always interested in nursing, and very often on my days off I'd spend quite a bit of time with the district nurse. It started when a friend's relation was having a baby and I helped at the birth with the Bowness nurse. When I'd finished I got my engagement ring off the mantelpiece to put back on, and the nurse said, 'Give him the ring back and come and nurse with me.' This was old Nurse Sawyer from Bowness and I said 'No' but afterwards I regretted it. I don't mean not finishing with my fiancé but not taking my certificate for nursing.

By this time I'd been working for six years and my wage had gone up from five shillings a week to seventeen shillings and sixpence. However my sister who lived at home was having a baby and they both died. I had to go back home because Dad, my brother and brother-in-law were on their own. They said, 'She'll have to come back, there's no one else.' I came home at the end of July, then at Christmas my brother decided he'd get married. I was disappointed because I could have stayed at Windermere. You see, the house at Kentmere wasn't big enough for two housewives. So my fiancé said, 'If they're getting married, why don't we?' and we decided to have a double wedding.

We were married at Kendal Registry Office in Lowther Street by old Mr Reid. In the office there was a big mahogany table with two brass candlesticks, a crucifix and a vase of flowers. Except for the prayers and music, we went through a full marriage service. It was beautiful. The four of us spent the day in Kendal before going to the pictures in the evening. In the afternoon, though, my brother and husband decided they would have a drink at the Golden Lion in the Market place. Us two ladies marched in with them and were ordered out. The landlord said, 'I'm sorry but we don't have ladies in here,' so we sat on the windowsill outside with a drink.

When we first married, we had 'rooms' in Staveley but I was ill and the doctor said I had to get away from the river, which we lived beside. As it happened, a cottage was advertised at Crook and we got that. It was a lovely old cottage but we had no running water when we first moved there. I loved that cottage where both my daughters were born and we lived there for fourteen years. The lady who owned the property let us have a smallholding which was seven and a half acres of ground. I set up a poultry farm with 400 head of poultry, and kept two pigs and a cow for our own milk. I also used to take some cows for the winter, as we had our own hay.

Dolly's husband (on the right) working on the road between Troutbeck Bridge and Ecclerigg, c. 1930

Not long after I was married, I visited St Monica's where someone I knew had had a baby. St Monica's was a home for unmarried mothers at Highfield in Kendal and, to be truthful, I never knew it existed or that these girls were looked after. In my home, when I was younger, it would have been, 'You've got yourself into that hole, get yourself out of it.' The two ladies who ran the place, though they were very good to the women, had no sympathy with them. So, as you can imagine, it was very, very strict. The women had to keep the place clean, scrub, do the laundry and look after their babies. There wasn't much tenderness for a woman in labour at those places, as it was looked on as a punishment for doing what they shouldn't. Relations could visit the women but you rarely saw them.

Usually the mothers stayed at St Monica's for about three weeks after the baby was born. Then a lot of the women looked for houses where they could go as a maid and take the baby with them. They would be kept apart from the family, usually as kitchen people, so they weren't in touch with their betters. A lot of the gentry had no sympathy. It was cheap labour to take a woman and child and she would usually stay, no matter what the conditions were like.

I offered to foster someone's baby as a friend but the authorities said, 'You can't do that. You've got to be registered as a foster mother or you can't have the child.' Thinking nothing of it, I registered, but I didn't realise that any more children the authorities had, they would ask if I would take them. In the end I fostered five altogether. As foster parents weren't so easy to get, I was paid five shillings a week. Mr Reid, the Registrar, was in charge and he came once a month to make sure that both the baby and I were all right. I think a lot of children were born out of complete ignorance. In the country districts, when illegitimate children were born, nine times out of ten the grandparents brought them up. That's why some people didn't really know who their parents were.

I delivered ever so many babies for neighbours. Before the war, you could deliver a baby without a doctor being present. Babies were born at home and, as most people had iron bedsteads, a rolled up towel was put through the rails at the head of the bed for the woman to hang on to. In those days, women always used to lie on their left side to have the baby delivered. You made sure there was plenty of old sheets under her and lots of newspaper beneath that. I know some people have a harder time in labour than others but you could soon tell if everything was all right. If it wasn't, you had to hurry the doctor up, though very often he had to cycle or come on horseback and couldn't be there in five minutes. In those days you had a piece of cloth about two inches square. This was folded into four and the middle cut out, then held in front of the fire until it singed brown. When the baby was born and washed, a penny was put in its navel, the singed cloth put over the penny and finally a binder was wrapped around. I learned ever so much from doctors. One said that he didn't believe in any woman being in labour more than eight hours and I quite agree with him.

One birth I attended was very difficult and the doctor asked me to stay with the mother. I stayed with her from twenty to seven on Thursday morning and didn't leave until four o'clock on Saturday afternoon. The baby died on the Saturday morning and I'll never forget that experience. I was sitting, talking to the lady, and the baby was in a basket by the fire. I just happened to glance across at the baby and I've never seen anything so peculiar in my life. It was as though the sun had been shining and a cloud came over the top of the baby. I knew it had gone and I just sat there. I didn't dare tell her. It was most odd. What caused it, I don't know. With religion, there's things we don't understand and never will.

A great part of country life in days gone by was reassuring people. I never let them think anything was wrong. A lot of infection was carried. You see, neighbours would be in and out of each other's houses, and, if one had an infection that was it. People very rarely went into hospital, they had their babies at home. Eventually, when they were old, they died at home and I wish I had five-pound notes for the number I've seen die. My husband used to say to me, 'You're more often in somebody else's bedroom than mine.' Well, if someone was ill and their family had been looking after them all day they'd ask me to sit up with the patient. I've never been afraid of death. I'm not really religious but it's part of life – you're born and you die. You can't go on living for ever. The worst part was to sit and see people suffer because there wasn't any painkillers, you just had to sit it out.

When someone died, you didn't send for the undertaker to take them away like you do now. You got a flat board or table with a cover on it and you laid the corpse on that. You hadn't to touch the corpse for three-quarters of an hour, as the impurities came away in that time. Then you plugged the extremities and washed them all over before putting a nightdress or pyjamas on them. A lot of people used to cross the arms of the dead, which is a very silly thing to do. You should put the arms down by their sides, because if you cross their arms the coffin needs to be wider. When the body was put into the coffin, it was kept open until the day of the funeral. In olden days the coffin was carried to church and a hearse was only used for any distance. After a funeral it was under-stood that there'd be a meal. Well, when you think about it, a lot of relations had to walk a long way. Lots of them couldn't cycle, and there wasn't buses so they had to walk.

The last war made a lot of difference. Everybody with land had to plough and all my eggs had to go to the packing station. Though we weren't supposed to, we used to sell the odd eggs to neighbours, as all country folk did. There was a lot of evacuees, mostly from Lancashire, in this area and they were very nice kids. I didn't have evacuees because I had the smallholding and was a registered foster mother, so I only helped at Crook School. We served dinners and made sure that all the evacuees got their meals properly because you always get the odd one who is very awkward. The meals were cooked on the premises – nothing fancy, just good sensible meals. And the country people round that district really looked after the children.

For a short time I got a job going round the area seeing that evacuees had settled in all right, which generally they did. But I went to one house and the owners had a mother and three children staying there. These evacuees were stuck up in one part of the house and only allowed to come down at certain times to the kitchen to cook. They were terribly unhappy. Well, I reported the owners, who weren't local I might add. They were people with plenty of money who just thought they were a better class and shouldn't have to entertain that family in their home.

What they didn't realise was that a lot of children's fathers were fighting the war for them. That was the only case I came across and they should have had more sense.

During the war my husband worked as a linesman for Manchester Corporation Water Works and in 1946 we moved to a house belonging to the company at Garnett Bridge. I missed Crook, as I had some lovely neighbours. In those days there was a friendly community in villages. It's a pity if it dies out but thankfully some villages are not letting it.

In 1951 we moved to Troutbeck Bridge and rented a house from the council. It was a lovely old house with four big bedrooms. One of the bedrooms was big enough to have two full suites of furniture, two beds and everything. All the other rooms were a fair size, so I did bed and breakfast and had quite a few regulars. One couple started coming when their son was nine years old. He's fifty-eight now and still keeps in touch.

There was a private house at Troutbeck and I used to go and look around the gardens. It was interesting to see how this house was altered to be made into the Cheshire Home. Then I got to going and doing odd jobs when people moved into the building. I'd go and help to wash patients' hair or help to prepare tea and wash up. It was while I was there that I got my Cadet Division of St John's Ambulance Brigade. So some of my cadets would come with me to the Cheshire Home to help. I think this gave the girls an insight into what life was like.

I joined the Windermere branch of St John's Ambulance Brigade in about 1952. It wasn't a very big organisation but it was very active. We went to Carlisle for meetings and demonstrations and all over the place on sports days and for different competitions. In summer we had a caravan on the prom at Bowness.

Things have changed tremendously for women since I was young but life was much simpler then. When I was in my teens, you could go to the pictures or to a dance and no one ever bothered you. If you were frightened, you just had to tell the police and there was no need to worry. I know women wanted independence but the discipline has been taken out of it. I think you get a lot of pleasure out of helping young people and teaching them. That's what's wrong today. A lot of parents and other people don't take enough interest in the young, and that's no way to bring them up.

I don't get out very far now, so I like listening to the programmes on Radio Cumbria, about the things we used to do, the different dialects and all the recipes. I especially like hearing about all the 'nature' cures. You see, I believe in a lot of these cures. They're marvellous and I remember such a lot about them. All these things need to be preserved, they ought to be, it's our heritage.

TEN

'If she smiled her face would crack'

ALICE (b. 1910) & AGNES (b. 1908)
Seaton/Workington

ALICE: Mining, that was all there was round here in them days. Dad was a Deputy at Siddick Pit until he had his accident. The tubs, they ran over his legs. He lost the use of them and was more or less in a wheelchair. He used the money he got from his accident to have a house built for us all.

Father at Siddick Pit before his accident

Dad helped to organise the building of our house at Seaton, which had a back kitchen, a kitchen (or parlour as we called it) and three bedrooms. The toilet was outside and that was my job, every Friday, to scrub it out. We all had our jobs to do as youngsters. You see, my mother had ten babies and I was the youngest, born in 1910, but only six of us lived.

We had a huge garden and my father kept us going with growing seedlings and selling them. Our garden used to be like a fair on a Sunday morning with people coming and buying these plants. There was border plants, tomatoes, rhubarb, celery, raspberries, blackcurrants – you name it, we had it.

We also kept a pig. And the slaughterhouse man, who lived in the village, came and butched it. Mother used to keep the pig's blood in the pantry to make black puddings. One time, my brother went into the pantry when it was dark for a drink of milk, and drank the blood by mistake. He vomited no end – it was an awful experience!

I was four when I started Seaton School, which was half a mile away. I remember the teachers were very strict and one day I laughed at something and was brought out in front of the class. The Headmaster swished my hand with this cane and I was humiliated.

AGNES: I was born in 1908 at Siddick but we moved to Seaton before Alice was born. I walked to Siddick School from Seaton, as Mother thought it was a good school and my older brothers and sisters still attended there. I remember when we were out of school, playing at dinnertime, and there was a great big German Zeppelin and it hung in the air over Siddick. Whether it was taking photos I don't know, but they reckoned it would be spying. It was a huge airship in a sort of net, and I gather it did drop bombs near Barrow.

Walking to Siddick School during the First World War, I used to see soldiers marching these prisoners of war along the road. I think there was a prisoner of war camp up Flimby or Maryport way and I was always a bit timid and frightened of all these men. One day, as these soldiers were marching along, a man appeared with a knife, shouting, 'Fixed Bayonets, Charge. Fixed Bayonets, Charge'. I ran helter skelter to the Mining Superintendent's house and told him what had happened. The Superintendent got his car and took this man to Maryport Cottage Hospital as he was shell-shocked. That stood out in my mind. It was terrifying when I saw that knife.

I don't think people realised how bad the First World War was. You see, there was a lot of hand-fighting and the men suffered terribly in the trenches. The next war was bad but it was cushy compared to the first one. The second war was still war and very frightening but they didn't have these awful trenches.

At school we put in a great effort for the war. We didn't have to but we thought it only right and we used to knit socks, gloves, mittens and squares for blankets. We were brought up to knit. Mother used to knit all our stockings and make all our clothes. When aunties were finished with their coats, she would turn them and make lovely coats for us.

Although we were poor we were always well-dressed, and at Christmastime we had nice velvet dresses. At that time of year, we had a Christmas tree but it wasn't called a Christmas tree like it is today. It was called a Christmas Bush and made from holly. The Kissing Bush was from a mistletoe bush. We used to hang our stockings above the black-leaded grate and get an apple, an orange, a new penny and a few little odds and ends. As we kept a few hens, we would kill one in the back yard for our Christmas dinner and always have a Christmas pudding with it.

ALICE: People used to do a lot more visiting in those days. On a Sunday night all my mother's sisters used to visit and then they'd come to let the New Year in. They would take the gate off and goodness knows where they would put it. Then you had to go and find it the next day and put it back. They would come and First Foot, bringing coal, money and salt. The coal was supposed to be lucky, salt meant not having to want, and money – well it was something you could always do with.

Dad was forty-eight when he died and Mother had to bring us up. I was nine then and Agnes was eleven. Mother used to go up to the village and do her shopping and only went to town [Workington] once a week, as she couldn't afford to go more often. There used to be a train running from Workington Central up to Seaton Station. When she came back, we'd meet her at the gate, saying, 'What have you brought us?' She always brought us a piece of apple pie and little things, like sweets.

Mother used to make a lot of what we called fatherless stews. It was sliced potatoes and onions fried in a pan, and that was your meal. Then, another time, we might have tatie hash with maybe a bit of corned beef in it. She used to make big slab cakes, a full tray because we were always hungry. Mind you, we always used to have good food and the oven was always on.

Most of the men in the village worked at the pits and our brothers went to Siddick Pit, just the same as Dad had done. My mother used to get up early to put my brothers out for morning shift and stay up when they went out. She'd be up by half-past four in the morning and when we came downstairs she had all the washing done. It was outside and hanging over the gooseberry bushes or anywhere she could hang it. There was accidents at the pits and a big one that my two brothers were in and quite a few were killed in that. A siren used to sound when there'd been an accident and women used to stand outside their houses wondering what had happened. It was a terrible time.

We had to buy our own coal, so Mother used to go down on the Siddick shore to pick it and bag it. When we came home from school we used to go down to the shore with a barrow and bring it home. As kiddies we used to play on Siddick shore, take a picnic of jam sandwiches with us and spend the day there.

AGNES: Women paid fourpence a week into the 'club' for the doctor. Dr Dudgeon was Mother's doctor, and when Dr Brown came back from the war he rejoined the practice. They were both splendid and would just come into the house, sit down and have a dish of broth if we were having some. Oh, that broth mother made in the set pot – everything went into it. There would be barley, carrots, turnip, a big lump of ham or a spare rib and, of course, all the stock. And the longer it stood, the better it got. The neighbours always got a jug full of it.

ALICE: As kiddies we played hoppy beds on the pavement, tops, rounders, or knock on somebody's door and run away. When bramble time came, we went and gathered brambles, didn't we? Then we had bramble jelly, bramble jam and bramble pie. Whatever was in season we had it. My mother made stacks of jam and didn't she have a lot of jam of all descriptions, even down to the humble rhubarb.

A good little fair came to the Cloffocks at Workington and then up to the Green at Seaton. It came to Seaton at the back end [autumn], and if Mother couldn't afford to let us go she'd make pans and pans of toffee for us as a treat.

AGNES: The Sunday before Easter was Carling Sunday. Carlings are like peas, only brown and harder. Mother would boil them and put pepper and butter on. They were really good with potatoes and meat. Then on Ash Wednesday we had potato hash. Our pasche eggs were always boiled with onion peelings because Mother didn't like dyes. When they were done, we polished them and used to go to Camerton and roll them down the hill outside the graveyard. And we always had Easter outfits, which were white dresses with sashes round, that Mother made.

Another thing that was home-made, was 'spring medicine' which was treacle and sulphur. Sometimes we had a big jug of lemon juice with tartaric acid in it and a bit of sugar. Mother used to say it cleared your bloodstream, which I'm sure it did.

I would have loved to have stayed on at school but Mother couldn't afford it. From Siddick School I went to the Higher Grade in town and that's where I finished my education. If you passed your exams you went to college but you had to pay for that in those days.

ALICE: I never liked school and we had to leave at fourteen. It was either decided for us what we would do when we left school or we had to go and look for a job somewhere. A job would be advertised in the paper, you answered it and went for an interview. That's how Agnes and I both went to Carlisle and worked at a big house at Scotby.

At Scotby our day started at half-seven in the morning and finished when the family had their evening meal at seven o'clock and we'd washed up. The family was only a married couple with two children but they entertained a lot and Agnes and I did all the work. There was no other staff.

We got up in the morning, put the fire on, got the family's breakfast ready and laid the table for the family coming down. When they were having breakfast they would give us what we had to eat from the food we'd taken in to them. After breakfast, Agnes and I would clear away, wash up, scrub the floors, and do the bedrooms and stairs. Every day there would be a different room to clean and the carpets were swept with a long brush and shovel. Then there was the meals to prepare. In those days they had a light lunch, afternoon tea and finally an evening meal.

As employers, they were very strict but all right. We had half a day off a week and had to be in by nine o'clock at night. I can't remember going far, just for walks. We never got home for Christmas, as we were working, but our employers would give us a Christmas present, which was usually five shillings. I was paid eight shillings a week and I sent nearly all of this home because Mother used to buy our clothes for us. I was always homesick but didn't manage to come back home very often because we couldn't afford it.

As I was cook, my wage went up to ten shillings after a few months. I remember making bread in a stone jam jar. The jam jar was well greased, and when the bread was baked it would just fall out. It used to be cut thin and they all loved that bread. The kitchen range was just an ordinary, big, black-leaded thing. Our employer used to go out shooting and I remember these awful pheasants he brought back and we had to hang them up until they went blue and then pluck them.

AGNES: I left Scotby and went to Kendal to work. I was at Mr Parkin's on Highgate and that was a very good place. Mr Parkin was a retired bank manager and a real gentleman. When he was ill I helped to nurse him, and later when he died I got a good 'handshake' and came home. I got £150, which in them days was a lot of money.

ALICE: I was at Scotby for about three years and then a friend, who was working in London, got me a job. So I was seventeen when I went to

Agnes in service at Kendal, c. 1930

work at Beckenham in Kent. It was only a small house that I went to and my wage for doing the housework was ten shillings a week. From there I moved to another place for three years before going to my final family in Beckenham. By that time, my wage was fifteen shillings and it never went up from there. I had myself to clothe and send my mother something out of that – five shillings every week I sent her. The Depression didn't really touch us down there and the last place I was at, they had a butcher's shop in Tottenham Court Road, which served all the hotels, so we were all right for food.

I still didn't get home very often and if I did come, it was on a cheap day return by train that cost £2.10 shillings. I had to set off early in the morning from Beckenham and was only home for an hour before starting back again. I never wanted to work at home [West Cumberland] because it was slave labour here compared with down south. We used to

113

go into London, to the pictures and shows, then go walking with boy-friends. We stood all night to see King George and Queen Elizabeth's Coronation and were right across from them when they went into the Abbey. People were more royalist then, and you went to all these things because they really were history. You see, when the Prince of Wales abdicated, people were very disappointed because he was the People's King, the Working Man's King and, of course, the aristocracy didn't like it.

AGNES: He was ordinary. I saw him when he came to Workington and I remember the old Queen Mary coming in a landau up Oxford Street and she sat so erect.

ALICE: If you had a close-up of her, you would think somebody had put flour on her face. It was all white. She never smiled, did she? We used to say, if she smiled her face would crack.

AGNES: When I came home, I started work at Mrs Hind's, the confectioner's down in Fisher Street, and lived there because it was handier. Mrs Hind was a leading confectioner in the town and used to make beautiful stuff. I worked in the shop and the café. In fact I went into the bakehouse and helped out with a lot of things. Oh, I can remember them huge steak and kidney pies, big roasts of pork, beautiful.

The Reds had a very good football team then and we used to do all the Reds' coffees, teas and whatever after the game. The teams they played all used to come back to Mrs Hind's for a meal before setting off home. Same with the rugby – Wigan and all these – they used to come to Mrs Hind's.

I managed to get home to Seaton twice a week, as I had one half day and one evening off, from five o'clock till ten o'clock. Mind, the wages were poor. I only had twelve shillings a week and later on it rose to fourteen shillings after four and a half years. That was the highest wage I ever had.

ALICE: Mr Cape, the Labour bloke, was the MP for Workington at this time and I used to know his daughter when we were both in London. We used to meet her father and he used to take us for tea on the terrace at the Houses of Parliament, which was very nice. Mr Cape took us round the Houses of Parliament and into the House of Lords. I didn't feel over-awed at all in those places, as I was with Mr Cape, who was a working-class man. He was very nice, very friendly and would listen to all your troubles. Workington always was a Labour place and it still is today.

Mr Cape's other daughter was an Alderman up here and then

Mr Cape, Labour MP for Workington, 1943, with his daughter (left) and Mrs E. Cain, Mayor (right)

Mayoress as well. I remember she took me with her when she was visiting the workhouse, somewhere at Whitehaven. How the people lived there, I do not know. The tables and chairs were scrubbed white and there was flagged floors and they only got the bare necessities to eat. You see, folk that couldn't get anything to eat, that had nothing at all to live on, used to be put into the workhouse. They were really just poor people, and many had been turned out of their homes. That's why they were there. One man that I know who was in the workhouse, he was a bit slow on the uptake. There was a lot of people like that in there. That's why there was so many tramps round here, they were people who were just poor. My mother never turned a tramp away, she always gave them a big mug of tea and a teacake or whatever there was.

AGNES: I was courting at the time with Billy who worked on the rail bank on the steelworks. That was the biggest industry round here at that time. Aye, it was a busy place. Billy had wanted to go to sea to be a merchant seaman but his dad wouldn't let him – he said it was too dangerous – so that's why he was on the steelworks. But it became very bad, very bad indeed. Part of the steelworks had closed down and other factories round here closed, so Billy was out of work. But he was lucky and got a job on the railway, at the railway blacksmith's shop in Stanley Street.

We got married in 1934 at St Michael's Church in Workington. My mother was living in town by this time and we lived with her. Believe me, Billy's wages were poor. When he got his taxes paid, we only had about £2 to live on, which wasn't much in them days, but he had a job. A steady job, that's all you could call it.

By the time the war came, I'd had pneumonia and pleurisy, so I was exempt from war work. But when the war started, that's when every-thing started looking up round here. Factories opened and everybody seemed to get back into work again.

ALICE: When war started, my mother said I had to come back home which I did. I went into the shell factory at Drybread, making shells. That was on Marsh and Quay which was a close community and they were nice people. I had to lift these 40 lb roughcasts on to the machine. On my first day I had to be massaged with olive oil when I came home because I was so stiff. Then I went on to a boring machine until the big shells were done away with. Then I was put on to a smaller machine. That went out and we went on to stripping plane engines.

A lot of people worked at the shell factory and it was a very friendly place – they were always playing tricks on each other. We had a union

Alice (centre), with her colleagues at the Drybread shell factory

Alice (left) and Agnes (right), 1940s

and I was asked to be secretary for a while, even though I'd never been political. There had to be unions to make sure you got your rights, whether there was a war on or not. There would be upward of 500 members and I just collected their money in, and if there was any disputes I would go in with the union representatives, see the management and try to settle it. The management would listen and you fought to get what you wanted. There was quite a few disputes at one time – wages disputes and one thing and another. Then there was accidents which you'd got to try and get 'compen' for.

When the war finished, I went to High Duty Alloys and was there for twenty-four years until I retired. I started on the shop floor where they made parts for aircraft. After three years, I got on to the staff and went into the planning department (what was called the 'Dream Room') where you used to type the layouts for the operations round the shopfloor. I finished up being in charge of the office. A few thousand worked at High Duty in those days and it was a good place to work.

AGNES: Seaton has been built up tremendously. The house where we were brought up stood on its own and there was about five other houses on one side and fields all round. Now there's council houses near and bungalows opposite and behind.

Generations change – there isn't the same friendliness as there was years ago. And there isn't many of us left in the family now. The first to go was one brother. There was no work here and he had to go away to Barnsley to work in the pits. He applied for the police force and was accepted but was drowned when he went swimming. He was eighteen, and a big, fine lad he was. Now there's only the two of us here and one sister who emigrated to Canada. The rest are all dead.

ELEVEN

'Dad had the miners' disease'

∽

JANE MUSGROVE (b. 1907)
Rowrah/Grange-over-Sands

There was a row of cottages at a place called Salter, which is near Rowrah. These were built when a new iron ore mine was opened and my parents would have been among the first tenants. In the early days these cottages just had a dry closet and an ash pit at the top of the garden. As time went on, water closets were put in, just across the back pathway. I think the cottages have been knocked down now, which is a shame.

I was born at Salter in 1907. My mother had a son and daughter already and lost two babies before I came along and then my younger sister. I'd be five when I was taken to what we always referred to as 'Road End' School because it stood at the crossroads but I think its proper name was Lamplugh Council School. One little girl had her left hand tied behind her back, to try and make her use her left hand. She used to cry and fairly break her back because she couldn't use her left hand. When I told my mother about this she said it was altogether wrong to try and make a child do something she couldn't do.

Dad was an iron ore miner at a nearby pit but when it closed down he had to find other work. Many years after the pit was closed, all the ground collapsed and this vast hole filled with water. An uncle told me that for hours afterwards the water still bubbled and churned in this hole. I think the water must have built up underground and that made the surface fall in. Now it's just a huge pond.

My mother's parents and brother lived at Salter cottages. Granny was a lovely old lady who was always knitting socks and stockings for herself or others. I never remember seeing her, other than she was working. Granda was a boss at one of the limestone quarries – I think it would be at Rowrah. A Mr Taylor-Swainson went round the quarries in a pony and trap delivering the explosives. They were kept in a locked building that only he had the key to.

We moved to Wath Brow and Dad started work at Jacktrees Pit at Cleator Moor, which was another iron ore mine. He always took his bait tin and bottle of tea to work. Then, when he was underground, he would take the cork out of the bottle and light a candle underneath it, to heat

Grandmother, c. 1910

the tea. In the iron ore mines, they worked by candlelight, as there wasn't the methane gas that was in the coalmines.

There was pit head baths which the miners used. But I always remember Dad scrubbed his teeth as soon as he came home, to get rid of the red ore dust, because they breathed it in through their nose and mouth. Then he used to go and use a pumice stone on his hands to try and

Granda (right) with Mr Taylor-Swainson

clean them a bit more. It was a job for my mother, washing Dad's clothes, because you couldn't get them free of dust no matter how hard you washed them. It was the same with the rough, hessian towels he used to scrub himself dry. Once Mother came down the garden with her washing, and when she was folding it up, she was a nappy short. She went out to look for it and found it lying on the path with a man's red clog mark on it. A passing miner had walked over it but no matter how many times the nappy was washed there was always the red mark on it.

Downstairs in our house at Wath Brow we had a sitting-room (or 'front end' as we called it), a kitchen, a scullery and a yard at the back with an outside WC. You went through the scullery to the coal house and the coal was delivered through a small door in the outside wall. The coalman opened this door, pushed the bags through and tipped the coal out. Mother always used to say, 'Don't leave that door open in the back kitchen because of the dust coming through.' You had to make sure the door was shut on the day the coalman was delivering, especially in summer.

On the kitchen range was what is called a 'rannel balk' in Cumberland. This was a hook and a bar up in the chimney that you could bring forward and use when cooking. You put the kettle or a broth pan with a big bow handle on to the hook. A drop bar came down that you stood ordinary pans on, over the fire. When we moved into the house there was a little side boiler but you couldn't keep water in it because it ran out. We only used it for kindling sticks, so that they were always dry.

'Dad had the miners' disease'

We had an allotment where Dad grew vegetables and Cleator Moor always had a good market on Saturday. I think there was also a smaller market on a Wednesday, when farmers used to come in their carts and sell produce. Further down the street where we lived was a branch of the Co-operative Society, so we never really went into Whitehaven much. The only time we went there was to visit my mother's sister and her husband who lived at Bransty. Uncle Jack was a postman in Whitehaven.

They were a mixed group of people who lived at Wath Brow, not just miners. The man next door to us was an insurance agent who travelled every day collecting money. Another house had a curious sort of family who never seemed to do much work of any kind. The old man at the house used to keep ferrets, and my father and him had leave to use a farmer's field for rabbiting. It cost fifteen pence in those days for two rabbits to feed a big family.

I went to Montreal School at Cleator Moor, which was beyond the marketplace, going down the hill. There was sections in the school for the infants, girls and boys. We used to go and peep through the keyhole into the boys' yard and talk to them. Oh dear, that brings back memories. Miss Sharpe, the headmistress, was one of the best teachers who ever lived. She seemed to take an interest in all the pupils. But if you'd been naughty you had to go and stand at her desk and get the cane. No other teacher was allowed to use the cane. I was fortunate enough never to have to go to her desk.

High Street, Cleator Moor, 1930s

Montreal School, Cleator Moor (Jane is in the back row, second from the right)

Inside the school was a closet where two pupils went to fill inkwells. For some reason I was there on my own one day, working away with the door shut, and I hadn't taken any notice of everyone singing 'Grace'. That was always sung before the school closed at dinnertime and everybody went home. I suddenly became aware that it seemed very quiet, and when I opened the door the school was empty! So I had to climb on to a box, open a little window and shout to a man who was passing to ask the caretaker to come and let me out.

In those days, if children were considered terribly poor or had a mother that couldn't really provide, they were allowed free milk and issued with clogs. But I think it was sometimes because the mother was a shiftless sort, who couldn't do as she ought to keep her family together.

My brother and older sister had started working before we moved to Wath Brow. He was an engine man at Ullcoates Mine at Egremont and my sister went into service. I remember coming pelting home after reading the telegram in the post office window, to tell my mother that the First World War had started. I knew my brother was of an age where he would probably have to go into the Army. My mother was upset about this and he did join up when he was old enough. I got some lovely silk postcards from my brother in France and he survived the war. At school, those pupils that were old enough knitted scarves and either fingerless gloves or mittens – I'm not sure which – as I know the soldiers had to have their fingers free for dealing with their rifles.

My younger sister and me did fairly well at Christmas, with having an older brother and sister. In our stockings there would either be a two shilling piece or a half a crown from them, which had to go into war savings. During the war one firm made chocolate figures about six inches high. These were dressed in crêpe paper uniforms of soldiers, sailors and nurses. We usually got one of those and it was something of a temptation not to eat them straight away.

When a couple got married, children used to gather around the house when the bride and groom were setting off on their honeymoon. As soon as the door opened, all the kids would yell 'Shill out, shill out', and the couple used to throw coppers which we'd scramble in the road for. If there was a gate leading to the house, the children would tie it so no one could leave without throwing the money. But, as a child, I mostly lived where there was terraced houses with no gates.

For a funeral, there was horse-drawn cabs and a horse-drawn hearse. I've seen an awful lot of cabs following a hearse. Men could walk but there was always room for people to ride. Years later, when I was back living in West Cumberland and it was a neighbour's funeral I drew my sitting-room and front bedroom curtains. People wanted to know why and I said it was just a habit. It had always been done at home when I was a child and you did it out of respect. If you were a family with children you didn't have your kiddies all gawping out of the window and maybe upsetting people.

It was taken for granted you would leave school at fourteen and go out to work, unless you were very brainy. There wasn't really any employment for girls other than going into the carpet mill at Egremont, as there was no real big houses for service. There wasn't much choice for the lads either. There was quarrying or going in the mines and the odd one would manage to get on the railway. I had always wanted to work with babies and small children and I did for a short time. A neighbour was a cook for some people on the outskirts of Lamplugh. These people had relations coming from abroad with a small child and wanted someone to look after it. So I went to Lamplugh for a while, and looking after this little lad was a joy.

While I was at Lamplugh I used to see the woman who lived next door and stabled ponies from one of the coalmines. It wasn't a deep mine where they went down in cages – the ponies walked in and brought bogies [carts] out full of coal. Wearing heavy tweeds and a tam o'shanter hat, this lady used to take a string of ponies to the pit every day and bring them back at night to the stables of the house where I was. I assume that the stables had originally been used by the staff of the house, but by the time I started working there the staff was reduced to just a cook/general.

Jane at home, 1926

My eldest sister had gone to a house at Windermere to be a cook and I joined her just before I was sixteen. I travelled by train and then up Windermere Lake on the steamer to Bowness. That was how you went to Windermere in those days, from this part of the world. It was the first time I'd been so far away from home but I wasn't really homesick, with my sister being near me. I thought Windermere was a lovely area and I enjoyed working at Heathwaite. My morning uniform was a blue cotton dress with a big apron and a cap like nurses wore. In the afternoon I had a smaller apron and a little frilly cap.

There was only my sister and me working at this house and first thing in the morning before breakfast we would clean the grates, put the fires on and tidy the rooms. Later there was the beds to make, and then my sister would get on with her work in the kitchen and I carried on in the front part of the house. My wage was five bob a week and more than half of it was sent home. You see, Mother had had to find the money for my uniform so I had to pay for it.

We had alternate Sunday afternoons off, a half-day a week and two weeks holidays a year. My sister only stayed there for about a year but I stayed on for about three years. I'd enjoyed working there and the lady of the house was nice but I wanted more money.

I moved to another place called Ibbotsholme, which was at Trout-beck Bridge. The house isn't there now, it's been pulled down. Inside was a big ballroom, kitchen quarters, staff sitting-room, parlour, maid's pantry, morning-room, dining-room, drawing-room and all the bed-rooms. All the lovely wood panelling in the billiard and games room is now in Carlisle Cathedral. The staff consisted of a cook, kitchen maid, parlour maid, house maid, and gardeners of course.

In my free time I would go walking, by myself mostly. I liked looking for birds' nests – not to pinch their eggs, just to be able to see them. I used to find their nests and go back when it was my following week's day off, to see if the eggs had hatched out. I've always been interested in wildlife. I remember as a very small girl going wandering on fine afternoons round the edge of fields, looking for nests. I'd be walking hand in hand with my mother and I remember how lovely it was to be lifted up to look into a bird's nest to see if there was eggs in it. There was no difference between the birds at Windermere and at home if you went to the right places to look. I love all birds and had favourites but I do think pewits are the most delightful little things when they're first hatched. My favourite walk was going to the top of Moor Howe and over into a field, walking by the stream where I could find little pink primulas, looking at the ground for birds' nests. I loved that part of the country, especially in spring.

It never bothered me being on my own because there didn't seem to be horrible things happening like there is now. I was very much a loner and even used to go way up Kirkstone Pass to find wild flowers and birds' nests. There is a perfectly good road that goes up there but it was a long slog. I didn't mind, I used to enjoy it. You could go walking locally and, other than Mr Rigg, there were no other people around. Mr Rigg was a gentleman from Windermere who had little Shetland ponies on the hills and sometimes you'd see him up there amongst the ponies, gathering them up and moving them, the same as you would a herd of cows. These ponies were moved down to a field at Winster and used to supply some of the mines. Mr Rigg was a heavy-built man who used to ride about on a pony. Some gentlemen with plenty of money had cars and a chauffeur but cars weren't as common on the roads as they are now.

I didn't manage to get home very much, just for my fortnight's holiday once a year. My father was out of work as the pit had closed but he managed to get another job at the Florence Mine and my parents moved to Low Mill near Egremont. I know that we sometimes used to be wakened by my father having awful nightmares and shouting. He had dreamed that he was fastened in the mine and there'd been a roof fall, or he was injured and he couldn't get out. It was awful to hear Dad shouting out in his sleep.

Dad had the miners' disease, silicosis, and he wasn't very old (about fifty-six or fifty-seven) when he died. He had seen other men suffering with this disease, he knew that he had it and he cursed it. Quite a lot of men from the mines got silicosis. It was pitiful to see him trying to do a little bit of work in the garden or walking any distance. A long time before my father died the doctor told my mother that if we could look into Dad's lungs they would be just like a solid block of stone. There was no treatment for silicosis, there was nothing the doctors could do. It was a shame really, that men had to die to make money for other people.

I next worked for an old lady who lived at Brathay. Oh, I liked Brathay because we were partly up on the hillside above the road. It was a nice place to work and rather quiet. There were three of us on the staff and we made our own enjoyment. There was a room on the first floor, which had belonged to the owner's husband, that we could use. This had been his work room, as he had done a little bit of joinery with tools and a lathe, though these were put away in a cupboard when we were there. We could go up there, to knit, sew or just sit and read, which was nice.

I'd been at Brathay for almost three years when the old lady unfortunately died. The staff stayed on after the funeral to clean and pack up the furniture which mostly went to the sale room. Brathay had been the nicest place I'd worked. The house looked down onto the river and the church and fells. From the back of the house, you could go on to the top of the fell. I used to sit up there and listen to the church bells on a Sunday morning instead of going to church. You could sit and think and meditate. I then went to work for an old gentleman at Windermere but came home when my mother was ill. That was the end of my life in service.

People, most of them 'townites', don't quite know what one did when one was in private domestic service. They're tickled to death when I say I was a 'gentleman's gentleman' or parlour maid. Besides waiting at table, I put out the gentleman's evening suit at night and put the studs in his shirt. The next morning I'd put the suit away again, having brushed it and seen there were no soup spills down the front or anything like that.

One good thing about being a parlour maid, you usually had a bedroom of your own. Mostly I was in a household where there was four girls, and after working together in the morning we each went off and did our own thing. After I'd dusted in the dining-room and laid the table for the next meal I cleaned the silver. This was done with wash leathers and rouge. I know rouge sounds like something you put on your face but it wasn't. It was more like iron ore dust to look at but you got a lovely polish on your silver with it. Staff worked at Christmas and I was usually given money as a present. This was always a help and sent home to my mother. In some houses we had a bottle of wine to celebrate with our Christmas meal, but, other than that, it was more or less just like any other day.

It never bothered me being in service, not in the slightest. One realised that there were working-class people and better-class people. You just mixed in and hoped for the best. The places where I worked, they were very good to their staff. I had heard of houses where they weren't so kind but I tried to avoid those. If someone was dismissed from a place they wouldn't get a reference. When that happened people turned to hotels, as they could get a job there even if it was only as kitchen staff without a reference. In those days there were quite a lot of girls from West Cumberland and Tyneside working in the Lake District. The girls from the North-East mostly went into the hotels rather than private service, as they preferred seasonal work.

I only had one unpleasant experience during my years in service. I'd been at home on my fortnight's holiday, and when I came back there was a curious atmosphere. I felt that I was being looked at with suspicion by other members of staff. I was friendly with a policeman at the time and I told him about it. 'Well, don't put up with it. Buttonhole the Missus and have it out with her,' was how he put it. In the end I did ask what was wrong and was told that I must have taken some silver home with me, as it was missing. Apparently the lady of the house had been sorting out various pieces of silver and put some in a cupboard and forgotten about it. I threatened to bring the police in because I wasn't a thief. I mean, we wouldn't have known what to do with this silver at home. Eventually she remembered where she had put the silver but I've thought many a time since what a fool I was to stay on. The other staff seemed so distant and it was a horrible feeling while it lasted. At the time I thought 'Everybody makes mistakes' and carried on.

My granny had died and my uncle came and lived with my mother. He had worked in the quarries but when he came to Low Mill he got a job on the railway. There was one item that always stuck in my mind about his job. In the three-cornered pocket where the sleeper and rail meet on a railway line, a pair of oystercatchers had their nest. Long before the men could hear the train coming, they used to keep an eye on these birds. I assume the birds could feel the vibrations, as they would toddle off the nest. This gave the men time to collect their tools so that the train could go through.

After Mother died, my younger sister and I bought a guesthouse at Grange-Over-Sands. The Second World War had started and there was a rule that there hadn't to be two women at home in one house. As my sister was married and had a little boy, I went out to work, travelling to Ulverston to work at Armstrong Siddeley.

Engines came to Armstrong Siddeley from aircraft that had been rescued from the sea. These had to be monitored carefully to make sure they were fit for use again. I don't know whether my job had a name – I just looked at certain parts of an engine for cracks. If you weren't certain, the part went to another bench where they checked it out. This work was different to anything I'd ever done before but I quite liked it. I was among a lot of nice young women and everyone was friendly. Occasionally we used to have entertainers and singers in the canteen at dinnertime, which was very enjoyable.

127

The hardest thing was getting to and from Ulverston, especially in the wintertime. I travelled to work by train but, as we lived midway between Grange and the next station, whichever way I went I had a long walk. So I was getting up about half-six in the morning and coming home late in the evening because the travelling added a lot of time.

The wives of some of the men who were working on the airfield at Cark used to stay at our house. These ladies came for holidays to be near their husbands but we didn't have many other visitors, with the war being on. Still, it was all grist to the mill. We were lucky really, as we had a very good butcher. When he found out that my sister was a good cook he would offer us bones to make soup with. And, if it's not giving away secrets, the manager of another shop was very good to us as far as cheese was concerned. You see, you couldn't cut cheese without it breaking up, so he gave us what he referred to as cheese crumbs – all these little pieces. Of course my sister could make all kinds of things that were cheesy, quite apart from giving us cheese on toast. I don't remember much about the end of the war, we were just glad it was over.

I married when I was at Grange. I'd known my husband for years and years, from when I'd worked at Windermere. We had a quiet wedding and went to Chester for our honeymoon. I remember we walked round the ancient walls and were interested to hear that, at a battle, someone with the same surname as my husband had stood shoulder to shoulder with the King. It chuffed me no end but my husband said, 'The silly bugger'. 'Oh Ted,' I said, 'Isn't it grand to think your ancestors were as loyal as that, that they fought shoulder to shoulder with the King?' All he answered was, 'Doesn't matter a damn to me.' But I felt quite chuffed about it, to think that everybody who walked round the walls of Chester was told this story in the commentary.

My husband was older than me and he decided that it would only be reasonable for me to be amongst my own people if anything happened to him. So we bought a house along the West Coast. I don't think there was any particular reason other than we both liked walking along the shore. We always did a lot of walking and had a car, so we could go further afield to walk. It's a nice area, I've made friends here. Yes, I like Seascale.

TWELVE

'He could only write his own name'

MARGARET PATTERSON (b. 1911)
Brough/Kirkby Stephen/Warcop

I was born at Brough in December 1911 at my grandmother's house. When I was three, my parents and I moved to a bigger house with some outbuildings and land where Dad kept some cows. This had originally been a doctor's house with a surgery attached, which was converted into a sort of kitchen. Unusual for those days, we had electricity and a bathroom. Brough had an electricity company and I think people could put in so much money and have shares. When the company was wound up the Electricity Grid had to buy them out, so people did very well out of that.

Brough School, c. 1904, where Mother taught

Stainmore School, c. 1906

My mother had been a teacher before she married – first at Brough, then at North Stainmore School. So when I started school at three years old I could already read. Brough school wasn't far away and about 100 pupils attended. There was two big classrooms and five teachers, three of them with the older children and two teachers with the infants.

I also went to Brough Sunday School and in summer we had a 'treat' that we all went to. We didn't go anywhere, as far as I can remember. We just seemed to go to Sunday School and have our tea. All the kiddies were handed a big bun that I could never get through – it was far too big. At Christmas, our party was held at the vicarage.

I remember the flour we used when the First World War was on. It was awful. People said barytes that used to be mined up on the fells was put into it. Barytes was heavy and so was the bread. I have vivid memories of the barytes mines up at Lune Head. Every Monday morning the miners used to walk to Lune Head, carrying all their bait [food] in a big clean flour bag, and they stayed up there all week in the biggish building which had bunk beds for them to sleep in. The barytes was brought down from Lune Head by carters who lived at Brough. Every morning they'd get up early, feed their horses, then set off to get a load, returning before midday. As Brough had a big steep hill, the carters put their brakes on and you could hear them squealing all the way into town. After dinner they walked down to Warcop railway station where the barytes was put into wagons and then the carters returned to Brough, fed and watered their horses, and that was their day.

Brough Peace Procession, 1919

Most people got the 1918 flu and a lot died then. Our local doctor worked almost night and day with that flu epidemic. Father got flu and Mother said the doctor often used to pop in about two or three o'clock in the morning to see him. In fact we all got flu and Father's turned to pneumonia. He was isolated and put into the front part of the house but then he got diphtheria.

The doctor wanted to send Father to the Kendal fever hospital. Mother said no, we could be kept at one side of the house while she looked after Father at the other side. We were all given an injection in our backs and I think a blanket was put up near where Father was. We hadn't to go past the blanket, which had Jeyes Fluid on it, until Father was better. Mother had once been to the fever hospital and once was enough. I've heard people say it was very stark – patients with scarlet fever at one side and the ones with diphtheria at the other side. Diphtheria was a real threat in those days.

When I was seven years old we moved to Granda's farm at Warcop. Granda was a character who had been born in either 1830 or 1831. His father had been the land agent for Lord Wakefield at Kendal, so Grandad went to school with Lord Wakefield's sons and the other gentry. He said he was up to some prank one day and the schoolmaster said, 'Now Lambert, remember you weren't born with a silver spoon in your mouth like these others lads.' When his father took over Burtergill (where his wife's relations used to farm at Warcop) Grandad left school and worked for him. Grandad was a very learned sort of man who won a

131

national prize by writing a book on farming that was published. If I asked him to help me with my maths homework he would do it in decimals. Then he'd say to my father, 'Well Rob, what have you got?' and Dad would work it out in fractions. While they were having this friendly argument, I'd have done my sums and gone on to something else.

I remember Grandad getting dressed up to go and pay the rent. Everything had to be aired and he would be fussing around and saying to the maid, 'Now, will you air me so and so?'

'Well, I'll air his stick for him and then he'll be satisfied' was the maid's response.

She would fetch his stick and he'd put his bowler hat on and, all dressed up, he'd walk down to pay the rent to the Lady of the Manor at Warcop Hall.

Living at Warcop was very different to Brough, and at Burtergill Farm we were out of the village altogether. The farmhouse had a great big kitchen with two tables. At the top of one table sat the shepherd, the horseman, the cowman and then the farm lad. They had a hierarchy and the shepherd was always the boss of the hired men. At the table, he helped himself first to the food, the others followed and the farm lad was last, even though there was plenty for everybody.

When we moved to Burtergill the farmhands had porridge, followed by bacon and eggs for their breakfast. But they had to eat the porridge up and then their tea was poured into the porridge basin for them to drink. At dinnertime, it was usual for the men to scrape their plates clean and have their pudding on the same plate. Mother altered all that and the men got a mug for their tea and a plate for their pudding. Very often, if there was a suet pudding – a real sticky suet pudding – you had that first. Someone once said that they thought it was to fill you up so that you didn't eat as much meat. But we were never short of meat because we kept a lot of sheep.

The farmhands had their own staircase and room, with it being a big farm. The young lad would be from the village and the others from further afield. Old Jack, the shepherd, was a real character. He could only write his own name and only read the *News of the World*, which he gloried in every Sunday. Jack was a local man who'd worked in the munitions at Barrow, and he went back there to stay with his niece for his term holiday. When Jack went to the 'Draught Yew' [ewe] Sales he didn't come back, as he always celebrated that night. These Draught Yew Sales at Kirkby Stephen were very important, as they provided local farmers with their money. Draught yews were sheep that were really too old for another hard winter on the fells and were sold to the lowland farmers who had better pastures for them.

I don't know how many sheep we had. You didn't ask people that because sheep was their wealth. Mother used to say that a good fat lamb did us for four days, and if she made sheep's head broth as well, that made another day. Both the family and the farmhands had the same meals. We'd have a cooked breakfast, meat and potatoes etc. for dinner, and almost always meat for supper. At most farms in those days, if sheep got fluke, and the shepherd caught them before they dropped, he would cut their throats. Well, the meat was good. It was just the liver that was bad and that was cut out.

When we were children we always got an apple, an orange and other small gifts at Christmas. But Mother had a friend who was a courturier and had her own business in London. She had made my mother's wedding dress and used to send us a decent Christmas present. I remember the boys getting meccano sets and I once got a Waterman's fountain pen and *nobody* had anything like that.

On Christmas Day, Father's sister and her husband, who had no family, came for their dinner. Seeing we had visitors, we would be in the big dining-room and we used the round table that would seat twelve of us. We always had goose for Christmas dinner and the farmhands in the kitchen had exactly the same. After the meal we would play cards, but one Christmas we were playing when somebody said, 'It's Sunday.' The cards were packed up immediately, although we were great card players. In winter we always got the cards out at six o'clock when we'd finished our supper. My parents were very keen on cards, or any game that used your brain, and Grandad taught all us children to play whist. We used the big kitchen table and there might be eight or nine of us, the men included, playing a game called Red Devil.

We spent New Year's Eve cleaning – everything had to be spotless. The brasses had to be cleaned, the darning basket had to be emptied (and you know what a darning basket was like in those days, with the menfolk wearing woollen socks). Just before midnight, mother would take the ashes out of the kitchen fire so that everything was fresh for the New Year. I think the idea was, if you made an effort for the New Year you carried on making the effort for the rest of the year.

For over a year I went to Warcop School which was just over a mile away, so I took a packed lunch. There was about seventy pupils there, with three teachers. After that, I went to the grammar school for girls at Kirkby Stephen and lodged with an aunt during the week, coming home by train at the weekend. While I was lodging with my aunt I used to go to the Band of Hope meetings. We'd be shown these slides, the first one showing this lovely home with a well-dressed family eating their dinner. The next slide would be of Father going to the pub and the family not

Bird and Arbor Day, Warcop School, c. 1905

looking so smart. This would lead on to the furniture being disposed of, Mother crying and Father drunk. A lot of people were teetotal in those days and there's still Band of Hope meetings.

There was a workhouse at Kirkby Stephen and people didn't like having to go there – it was a much-dreaded place. But there was no old age pension then, and when it was introduced it would be ten shillings a week for people over seventy. The men in the workhouse were too old and feeble to look after themselves and they wore corduroy trousers that had been washed until they were almost cream-coloured. These old men were always very clean and they chopped sticks which they sold in bundles.

I think my parents paid about £4 a term for me to attend the grammar school. Later, when my sister joined me, it would have been less, though there was still our train fares and uniform to pay for. With my sister at the grammar school, we travelled every day by train, as a lot of the girls did. The trains ran from Penrith to Kirkby Stephen and two trains ran each way, five times a day. Kirkby Stephen was a junction for trains from Darlington and one that ran down to Tebay and that area. It was a busy station then and there was even a refreshment room.

The discipline was strict at the grammar school but it didn't do us any harm. No one was ever in trouble, except the girl who had her hair bobbed one weekend (the headmistress didn't like that). We all wore a gymslip, white blouse and black stockings. You couldn't wear a cardigan in winter and there wasn't any thermal vests to put underneath the blouse. We also wore lace-up boots in winter, and when the General Strike was on there was no coal for the school stoves and it was so cold that we all got chilblains.

The lessons at school were very different from Warcop and we had algebra, geometry, Latin and French. Once a year we had a speech day and there was a prize for a pupil from each class. I got three prizes during my time, so I think I did very well. I would love to have stayed on at school, as I wanted to be a doctor, but there was no grants in those days. So I left school at sixteen, as my mother wanted me at home, and I worked on the farm for half a crown a week.

The first big event of the year was lambing time and that was busy as we had a lot of sheep. We also kept a couple of pigs, some cows and hens for our own use. The five or six horses we had were big Clydesdales and there was a black Galloway pony for Grandad to ride about on (he would have been in his late seventies then). This pony was a bit slow and Grandad always kept a safety pin in his jacket to give the Galloway a poke with.

In June all the farmers set a date for clipping the sheep and gathering them off the fells. Now that was a big day. Mother would order a round of beef and a ham and bake for a long time beforehand. I remember the ham, as she used to cook it wrapped in a flour and water paste. The cooked ham was served cold and the beef hot. There could be up to thirty people, including relations, to help out with the clipping. Father bought a nine-gallon barrel of beer, and at intervals you took it round for the men to drink, as clipping was thirsty work. Home-made lemonade was also taken round for those who didn't drink beer. At dinner time we always had the roast beef with vegetables, and trifle for a pudding. Years back, the tradition had been for plum pudding but Father said this was too heavy and asked for something lighter. There'd be tea to prepare and many would stay for supper so it all took quite a bit of organising. Elderly relatives who weren't doing anything helped by cleaning the silver and putting it away.

Haytime would be straight after the clipping and that's when you needed the horses. It took a long time in those days because there was no machinery. The hardest job was raking the hay from the back of the dykes, which the women did. If the men were working away from the farm, sandwiches, rock buns, pastry, cakes, fruit loaf and a can of tea would be taken out to them. At harvest time you wanted the horses again, because it took three of them to pull the binder which cut the oats, while we had to stook the corn. Sometimes it rained and the stooks had to be taken out, shaken and put the other way round to try and dry them out. Then it was all to put into stacks, and during the winter the stacks were threshed.

We kept Shorthorn cattle for their milk and made butter once a week in a great big churn. The buttermilk would go to the calves and pigs and the butter to a grocer at Kirkby Stephen. In about 1934 Express Dairies started up near Appleby and began collecting milk. That was when we changed from making butter to selling milk.

We never had any bother with gypsies on the farm, though I suppose Father looked out for them in the fields. The gypsies came for Brough Hill Fair and I know it sounds daft but the fair is held in Warcop. I understand that it had been held at Brough a long time ago, and when there was a plague it moved to Warcop but still kept its original name. Before my time it was a real big fair, a proper gypsy fair, when they all came by horse-drawn caravans from everywhere. It's dying out now and only a few caravans come but people still say 'It's Brough Hill weather', meaning it's getting winterish. That's because the fair is held at the end of September beginning of October.

There was plenty going on in the village – there was the Women's Institute for one thing. Mother was a founder member of the village WI, and after leaving school we joined as soon as we could. I can remember my mother going to all sorts of cookery classes – they'd never had anything like that for women before. There was embroidery classes, lectures on health, glove-making, curing rabbit skins and they even bought a marmalade machine which women used to cut their orange peel. Mother learnt an awful lot – she was all for learning – and it filtered back to you. If a newcomer came to the village and joined they were in a happy band of people. There weren't any cars then, of course, but you made the effort to attend, otherwise you wouldn't see others from the outlying districts. Yes, the Women's Institute was a boon, it really was.

The Lady of the Manor, Mrs Wilde, took a big part in village life. She was the Church Warden, President of the WI, and everything that was going on, she would be head of. You definitely knew she was the Lady of the Manor but she was very good. It was always 'Have your meetings in my Gun Room' or 'Do you want any tea or sugar for whatever you are doing?' Mrs Wilde took a great interest in young ones and provided a room where we could meet for the Girl Guides and also tea after the Rush Bearings. We still have the Rush Bearings, where the girls carry garlands of flowers and the boys have their crosses of rushes. The children walk round the village and leave their offerings of flowers and rushes at the church. After the church service there's tea and sports, which are well supported.

The Reading Room was well used. It had a billiard table, daily papers to read and a fire was put on every night. Once a year, at the Annual General Meeting, men could bid to buy a paper. This meant that when everybody at the Reading Room had finished reading that particular paper, you could take it home, as you'd bought every edition for the year. A lot of the farm lads used to go there. It was a place where they could all meet, an alternative to the pub.

For a funeral at Warcop, they used a hearse that's now in the Abbot Hall Museum at Kendal. It's just a very basic affair but I can remember it being pulled by a black horse and the driver sat up high in front. Out of respect, the driver wore black and a black bowler hat. I'm sure the church bells were rung when somebody died. I can't remember how they distinguished if it was a man or a woman by the bells, but we knew. Then there was so many peals for their age, but all that went out a long time ago. Undertakers didn't come when there was a death. Instead, a lady who was known to do 'laying out' was sent for. The body was kept at home in the coffin, and if you visited the house you would be asked, 'Do you want to see so and so?'

My brothers worked on the farm after they left school and I stayed there until I got married. I met my future husband at some local function and got married when I was twenty-three. My wedding dress was white velvet and our reception was held at home in the big kitchen. For our honeymoon we stayed with some friends of my husband's at Liverpool and had a great time, as it was January and there was all the pantomimes to see. We went to the Argyll Theatre at Birkenhead because that was where all the artistes used to try out their acts before going to London in those days. I remember we went to one of the big shops, Owen and Owen's, for afternoon tea and it was one and sixpence each.

My husband was a farmer and we took over a farm that happened to be vacant when we married. It had a good big house that was rather smart and had getting on for 200 acres, so we had two men working for us. We were living there when I had my children. In those days when you were having a baby you got a monthly nurse and she did everything. She didn't let you put a foot out of bed for ten days after the birth. Women visited the doctor to have it confirmed they were expecting and didn't see him again until he was sent for. The doctor came for the birth of the baby and the monthly nurse carried on. This lady wasn't a trained nurse, just a local woman who did that job, and you had to book her up beforehand. From what my mother said, I don't think that having children had altered much from her day. All my children were born at home, except the last one that I had at Penrith Hospital.

When a baby was baptised, some vicars preferred the mother to be 'churched'. At the baptism of my first baby the vicar asked me if I would go with him up to the altar. We went and said a few prayers. Just a sort of thanks for a safe delivery, that's all it was. Nobody made a fuss about it. It wasn't 'You must go' or anything like that. But I don't remember this happening with any of my other children.

During the war in 1942 the Army came to Warcop and bought all the property that belonged to the Manor. At a month's notice, the people had to get out of their tenanted farms. It was a bit of a shock for Dad, as his family had been at Burtergill for more than 100 years. But the Army kept saying, 'There's a war on. It's compulsory purchase and you've just got to take it.'

We grew a lot of potatoes during the war, and oats because we had to feed our own cattle as there was nothing we could buy in. When we were short of labour we sometimes had to make do with prisoners-of-war from a camp at Burrells, just outside Appleby. We'd be asked how many prisoners we needed for potato picking and each morning they came by wagon. The Italians weren't very good workers but the Germans were. Often the Germans had been farmers or farm workers before the war and had nothing to do with the politics. My sister and her husband had an elderly German farmer on their farm, and he was a good worker. After the war, when he went home, my sister's family kept in touch with him. They went over to see him quite a few times and his daughter has been here.

During the war we bought a second-hand tractor, which was a great help. We more or less had to get this tractor, just to keep up with the demands from the Ministry. The main idea was that I could drive it and that spared a man but actually it was a lot easier driving than doing manual work. Sometimes I had a maid, if I could find one to help out with the children. You see, a lot of girls went into the services or went to do munitions work at Sedbergh. For a while we had a land girl who was really useful. She was from the Newcastle area and her brother was evacuated to Warcop.

The house that my sister later lived in was filled with evacuees who had two ladies in charge of them. The evacuees were from Newcastle at first and then Barrow. They went to the local school but eventually there was so many of them that they couldn't all be accommodated. When that happened classes were held in the Temperance Hall. Later, some drifted back home but a lot stayed for a long time. Oh, they loved it here and it's surprising how many of them come back just to have a look around. They say, 'Oh, we've just come back to see the place' or 'I've fetched the family back to see where I was evacuated.'

After the war, the Army took on the responsibility of providing the band and refreshments for the Rush Bearing. There's still big crowds to

Brough Brass Band, 1910–12

watch the ceremony and anybody who's carried a garland will try and come back to watch. Afterwards there's sports for the children, with wrestling and cups to be won. It's really well organised.

Warcop hasn't changed much over the years. There's a few new houses and four farms, whereas years ago there would have been a lot of small farms. We all look out to see if anyone's blinds aren't drawn in the mornings. If they aren't, two or three of us go and see what's happened. It might be that they've just slept in but it's better to find out. I've never wanted to leave Warcop and people round here are still very close.

THIRTEEN

'We're a very close-knit family'

GRACE PETRIE (b. 1922)
Salterbeck/Harrington

I was born at my grandma's house in Yeowart Ville, Workington, in 1922 but moved down near Sheerness when I was young. You see, my dad was in the Royal Artillery and we moved to Army quarters. I can't remember much about the place except that there was no street lights, and if we needed the doctor we went by boat over to Sheerness.

Dad was from Broughton originally and quite a lot older than Mam. He served in the army for twenty-two years before he retired and we came back to Workington. I'd be about ten when we came back and by that time there was six of us children. Dad served abroad, and every time he came home he left my mam pregnant. Eventually there was six girls

Grace with her parents, c. 1922

Workington Market, c. 1910

and three boys. We lived with Grandma again but, as her other daughter and son-in-law were living there, you can imagine how packed it was. Some of us slept next door at a relation's house on 'shakie downs' [makeshift beds on the floor].

Grandma was quite religious. She'd had two sons and two daughters, my mother being the eldest and auntie the youngest. They said it was like being brought up by two different mothers, as my mother was brought up before Grandma was religious. Once she was a practising Christian, it was a different lifestyle for my auntie.

There was no work for my dad. He used to get up every morning and go to Moss Bay Steel Works and some mornings he got an odd shift until eventually he ended up getting a job on the gantry. That was between Salterbeck and Moss Bay shore. Dad also used to go to the Town Hall about a council house for us. At the finish he got sick of going and threatened to pitch a tent outside their offices. It must have worked because we got a house at Salterbeck and Dad used half of his Army pension to furnish it.

When we moved to Salterbeck it was top and tail. The house had three bedrooms. Mam and dad had the front one but there was always a baby in with them. Us girls had the middle room, sleeping top to tail, and the boys had the smaller back room. The bathroom was downstairs and Dad used to bath us. We were put in the bath three at a time on a

141

Grace as a little girl, with her cousin

Saturday night and Dad washed our hair. He always used a small tooth comb, and when he put his hand on top of your head it was like a clamp, as he was such a big bloke. That's about all he ever did in the house. I don't think he could knock a nail in straight – my mam did everything.

With spring-cleaning, my mother had to do it in bits when Dad was out. She had to straighten everything up again for him coming home, then dismantle it and carry on the next day. He was a strict father and you didn't really have any conversation with him. When we grew up and asked him if we could go to a dance, if he said 'No', it was 'No'. It was only a lot later that the youngest lass got any freedom. When she asked if she could go to a dance, Dad didn't answer straight away but said to Mother later, 'You can tell her she can go.' My sister said, 'I'm not going to the dance now, but in future if I want to go I'm going and not asking you.' From that day, if she wanted to go she just went and that was it. None of us older ones would have done that. In those days you didn't answer back – you were seen and not heard.

We were poor, and if family allowances had been on the go my mother would have thought she was a millionaire. You got nothing at all. You had your family, that was your responsibility and you just had to get on with it. I've known her not have a penny for the gas – she had a very hard life. In fact we couldn't afford gas so we used candles. I remember, we used to have one pair of socks and one pair of knickers each, which we washed and dried on the mantelpiece for the next day. I was washing my socks in the back kitchen and I must have knocked over the candle, setting the curtains on fire. I ran next door but I got played pop with when I came back.

I used to go to the butcher's for threepennyworth of 'cuttings'. These were just bits of steak or mutton for mam to make stews with. Then with pig's trotters she made her own brawn, and with a sheep's head it was broth, which Dad would pick at when it was cooked and eat the brains. Cow heel was was another thing that they had a lot of, with salt and vinegar on, and Mam did like tripe and eels. I've seen my mother walk to town with two babies in the pram and two kiddies walking with her, just to get cheaper vegetables from the market. But it was wholesome food that we lived on – you could get a rabbit for tenpence.

There were no gas ovens then, just a side oven beside the fire, and it was marvellous how they could regulate the heat. Mam made her own bread and one time when she was in bed, after having a baby, she was shouting instructions down the stairs as Dad was trying to make the bread. He forgot to put the salt in and we had to eat it. You can guess what bread's like without the salt. Ugh!

All women stayed in bed for a fortnight when they had a baby but they didn't have a doctor unless they needed to be stitched. They prepared for a birth a lot more than they do now. Newspapers were saved to put on the bed, and when the baby was born the afterbirth was always burnt on the fire. It was just something they always did. Then a penny was placed on the baby's navel and a binder put round it. Even the women wore binders. Babies wore a lot more clothing then. First they had a vest on, then a barrow coat, which was as long as a nightie but sleeveless. On top of those was the nightie and a little coat. I think Mam paid sixpence a week to cover her in case any of us needed the doctor. Above Crellin's sweetshop at Harrington was where Nurse Richards, a little Scotch nurse, lived. When any mother went into labour the children would go and knock for Nurse Richards to come. If it was through the night, the two eldest children would go for her, as me and my sister did.

Harrington was a busy little place then. There was a butcher's, a jeweller's, barber's, Co-op, fish and chip shop, police station and quite a lot of churches and pubs. We used to take a tin of jam sandwiches and a bottle of water and spend many an hour on the shore. It was a cheap pleasure and we couldn't afford anything else. Even when I had a family of my own, we spent good days on the shore as everybody did.

Salterbeck was a good little community with its own policeman, Mr Glaister. We even had a fair-sized carnival – everybody got involved in it. Mrs Wordsworth made our costumes and there'd be decorated lorries

Church Road, Harrington, c. 1930

and floats which went along the Front Road, down Walls Road, and round the Oval. We all got a bag with something to eat inside and then the sports were held in the field where the cemetery is now.

Of course a lot of the houses at Salterbeck were only built after the war and there was a lot of fields. Down at the bottom, where Pearl Road is now, was Wilson's farm. They used to deliver milk by horse and cart and we'd get our fresh milk in a jug. The milk on the cart was in a big container, with a tap that you turned for the milk to run into your jug. One of our lads forgot to turn the tap off when he got our milk. He didn't half get played war with, as there was milk everywhere on the street.

The one thing parents were strict about was going to Sunday School. Poor as we were, we went to the Gospel Hall at Moss Bay every Sunday afternoon. I went to St Michael's School when we came back from Sheerness, and as we got older, most of us girls went to Victoria School. For swimming lessons we went to the public baths and Mam made our costumes from jumpers. As you can imagine, when you came out of the water the swimming costume would be down to your knees! I was still at school when I joined a girls' choir at High Harrington and we entered musical festivals. The music teacher gave me a dress, which had probably been her daughter's. It was all lace and frills, tiered right down to the ankles. Oh, I thought I was the Queen Bee in that dress.

I left school when I was fourteen and went into service right away. I went for an interview at Vulcan's Lane in Workington for a job at Heversham Grammar School. When you were going away, the first thing your mother did was buy a pair of corsets to take with you. Those fastened under the bust and they used to dig in something terrible but you automatically wore them in those days.

I travelled by bus to Keswick, then to Kendal, before arriving at Heversham Grammar School. When I got there, I remember saying 'Yes Ma'am' or 'No Ma'am' to whoever was showing me around, and when all come to all it was the Matron. Oh, she was strict and you always knew when she was around because you could hear her keys jangling. Our bedroom was out of the big house and up some wooden stairs (maybe they'd been stables at one time). All of us, except Cook and Matron, slept in separate beds in this room and it was very cold in winter.

We had to provide our own uniforms which were blue with a big apron in the mornings and black with stiff cuffs and a little apron for the afternoons. My wage was seven and sixpence a week which was paid monthly. I sent money home, so by the time you bought a packet of sanitary towels you couldn't afford to go anywhere on your day off. I was an in-between maid and it was a six o'clock start helping in the kitchen and doing so much work in the dormitories. As it was a boys' school, you had to lock yourself in the dormitories when you were working in case any of the boys came upstairs.

When Doris the kitchen maid was leaving I was asked if I'd like her job. Well, it was the kitchen maid's job to make and knead a stone of bread and, as I was only little, I didn't know if I could cope with doing that. Mind you, I did want the job, as it was a shilling a week extra, so I was given a trial. Well, I put all my heart and soul into making that bread and I got the job. That was a bit harder for me, as twice a week I had to scrub the kitchen floor, which was all stone flags, and then clean the pantry. As you came in the kitchen door, there was a shelf and it was my job to put two tin plates on it. One plate was for a square of butter (that was divided into six for the staff) and the other was for our dry tea. With the draught, I've known the tea blow all over the butter.

I'll never forget the first chicken I had to pluck and clean. I was frightened to touch it and eventually tried to pull out one feather at a time. I actually tried to clean it with a spoon and fork, as I was frightened to put my hand inside it. The first egg I ever got out of a chicken, Matron took it off me. So, after that, if there was ever an egg in a chicken, I'd hide the egg under a pan which was kept upside down on a shelf.

You see, for food it wasn't a very good place. I can remember scrubbing the cellars out, where they stored apples in straw and eggs in a water glass. After scrubbing, my water was as black as black but I put my hand in the water glass, got six eggs out and put them in the dirty water. We had scrambled eggs that night. Another thing we did, when the home-grown tomatoes had to be weighed before selling them, we usually managed to pinch one, shove it up our knicker legs and make a sandwich with it later on. So the tomatoes would be underweight when they were sold to a shop at Kendal.

It was when I was the kitchen maid that I slept in one morning, and in my hurry to catch up I carried too many breakfast plates. Clatter, clatter, clatter! Matron spent all day trying to piece them together to see how many were broke, as I had to pay for them. So I gave my notice and wrote to my mother, telling her what had happened. She wrote back telling them not to accept it.

When the boys were on holiday from school we had to spring-clean. All the carpets were dragged out on to the grass and beaten. It taught you the rights and wrongs and was good training. The boys at the school were quite nice. There was one from Workington and I actually met him a few years ago. He's a Minister now and he came visiting at a hospital where I was a patient. I introduced myself and we had a good talk. He said to me, 'If you ever see me again, just say "Heversham".'

I'd been at the school about two years when I applied for a job as a cook at Levens Vicarage. I had a rise with that job and my wage went up to about eight shillings and sixpence. The first thing I was asked to do was make a chocolate cake and I wouldn't tell you what it was like. I'd never made anything like that before. It had always been vegetables and suchlike. But I learnt from my mistakes. Now, that was a good place for eating and the hours weren't so bad, as I got more time off in the afternoon. It was the Reverend Bannerman and his daughter who I worked for and both of them were very nice. In fact I was confirmed at Kendal Parish Church through the Reverend Bannerman.

It was while I was working there that the Prince of Wales abdicated. The Bannermans were out for the night and the staff went into the drawing-room without putting lights on and lay on the floor to listen to the abdication speech on the wireless. I started courting about this time with a chap who lived nearby. He was a Catholic and he took me home but his dad put me out of the house because I wasn't their religion. That romance dwindled away.

After the Vicarage I worked at Sedbergh School as a kitchen maid, then moved to the Fleece Inn at Kendal as a waitress, before moving back to Workington. You see, in those days you just kept moving to another job that paid more money, as you always sent some of it home. At Workington I worked for Dr Hodgson at Park End Road as a cook but when war broke out I went to Moss Bay and worked at the Shell

Grace in her WRAF uniform

Forge. I was on sand blast (which was blasting the shells) and it was either stopping there or going into the forces, so I went into the forces.

I joined the WRAF and had to report to Carlisle. There we all were with our gas masks in little cardboard boxes on our shoulders, carrying our cases and trying to march. We'd had no training, so what a laugh that was, marching from the recruitment office down to the railway station, trying to keep in step.

I was sent down to Wiltshire to train as a wireless operator, which I enjoyed, and then to various other camps. One of my worst memories was of the lass in the next bed who committed suicide. She was on a charge for taking officers' clothes coupons and took an overdose of tablets. It was a pity, as she was a married woman with two children and her husband was in the Navy.

Down at RAF Rafton in Devon was frightening. It was Coastal Command, mostly Australian and Canadian aircrew, and it was very upsetting when you knew the lads and they never came back. I've actually seen aircraft blow up before they flew off the station. The people from Scotland got an extra day's leave when they were going home because it was so far away. But, even though I lived way up here, I didn't get the extra day. It was a long journey, coming home or going back. Sometimes you never got a seat on the train – you were in the corridor sitting on kit bags – and the stations were always packed. But there was always somewhere on the railway stations where you could get something to eat or drink.

It was at a dance, doing the Hokey Cokey, that I met my future husband. He was in the Air Crew and later got posted to Four Group. We got engaged after six weeks and married six weeks after that. My husband used to get leave every six weeks and I only got it every twelve weeks. One time when he got leave I said, 'I'm coming with you,' and signed out of camp and then went absent without leave. We were at my mother's when we saw the military police from Silloth come to the door. My husband darted into another room while I lay in bed and said to the police that I couldn't move because of my bad back. I did go back to camp and signed in, so they couldn't charge me with either breaking in or out, but I was told I'd be on a charge the next morning. Before that I went to the Medical Officer, and he found I was pregnant. That meant I was 'unfit for all duties' and they couldn't put me on a charge. All I had to do was sign in at the guardroom and within two days I was discharged and sent home. So, really, I got no punishment for my absence without leave.

I went to live with my mother and I think, with having a big family, she gained in a way during the war. For instance, she could swap sweet coupons and suchlike for something else. I know we had to queue like everybody else but, on the whole, we coped. At the start of the war we got a steel nissen shelter put in the kitchen and we used it as a table besides using it when the bombs came. When the war finished every street round here formed a committee and had a party, with jelly for the kids and dancing in the street.

Shortly after my husband was demobbed, he got a job as a gamekeeper for Lord and Lady Mountain and we moved up to Dunkeld. We had a house on the estate and had visitors from home nearly every week. In fact two of my sisters got jobs as maids with Lady Mountain. In those days girls still wore ankle socks when they left school and Lady Mountain would comment to me that when going into dinner she could see one of my sister's feet and ankle socks peeping from under a curtain. You see, gentry used to dress for dinner, with the ladies in long dresses, and my sister would hide behind these big curtains to watch them all going in for their meal.

My health wasn't very good at this time and we moved back to Salterbeck and my husband got a job at Chapel Bank. A lot of the old customs hadn't yet died out. People still used to congregate in Central Square for midnight on New Year's Eve. No matter where they were, that's where they'd meet up at midnight. It was the custom to visit folk, go round the houses at New Year and take a drink with them. There wasn't much whisky then, maybe just cider, and people would have sandwiches prepared for callers. Now, of course, if people go round visiting, they don't have a drink with them – it's the occupants of the house who supply it.

People still washed and laid folk out at home and I've done that. The only one I couldn't do was someone's baby. I went round for my mam to do that. In them days, being neighbourly, after you'd laid somebody out, you'd fetch all the bedding home and wash it.

Even though there was work after the war the wages weren't very high. An awful lot of women, myself included, were waiting for their husbands to come home with their wage packets on a Friday night. As soon as he came in, you were out shopping for food. Most women would only get out once a week to the pictures with female relations or friends. If your friend couldn't afford the pictures one week you'd lend her the money, and she would do the same for you. Men usually went out for a pint on a Saturday night and the wireless was a wife's entertainment. Oh, I used to enjoy that, the kiddies in bed and sitting with my knitting and there was some good programmes on the wireless.

We've always been members of the RAFFA Club for ex-servicemen, and gone to the Group Four reunions. One year my husband was given the list for the reunion and saw that Guy, his old pilot's name, was on it. Well, my husband wrote to him and got a reply back from Sir Guy, as he is now, and then a phone call asking if we'd like to go to the Grosvenor House Hotel in London for 'Butch' Harris's eighty-fifth birthday. 'Don't worry about anything,' said Sir Guy. 'You can stay with us.'

I didn't know what to take and took far too much. We travelled down by car, with me in trousers and then changing into a costume between the two car doors in Windsor Great Park. When we arrived I got out of the car and said, 'Pleased to meet you, Sir Guy.' 'It's not Sir Guy, it's just Guy,' he answered. And his wife came up to me and said, 'I've just this minute put fresh flowers in your bedroom.' I just thought, 'Oh, my God.' I wouldn't say I've had a rough upbringing but, being working class, I do know how to behave with the right kind of people and we had a lovely time with them. They took us round London on the Saturday morning and the dinner that night was an experience. We met Sir Winston Churchill's grandson and the Duchess of Gloucester. It really was lovely.

Coming from a big family, we've all been very close to each other and were very close to my mother. After Dad died, we all used to meet every Thursday at Mam's or meet each other individually. Then, when Mam died, we took turns going to each other's houses and included my mother's sister. There's always somebody who'll help you or who you can turn to. I'm not saying we didn't fall out at times but we've stuck together. We've all got on and we still do. We're a very close-knit family.

FOURTEEN

'I'm part of Maryport'

ANNIE ROBINSON (b. 1905)
Maryport

My family goes back almost to the beginning of Maryport and we were a big seafaring family. In those days all my relations lived 'down street' near the docks, as everybody did, because there wasn't much 'up street'. But gradually they worked their way up into what was called the Town. They first lived in King Street and eventually moved to John Street, which had been built by my great-uncle, John Hardy.

Left: Granda Tweedie, Annie's maternal grandfather
Right: Grandma Tweedie, who ruled the household

I was born at Senhouse Street in October 1905. There was no hospital and women had their babies at home (they were all breast-fed in those days). Mrs Jackson the midwife brought me into the world and stayed for a month to look after my mother. Babies wore 'barrow' coats, or long clothes, at first. Then, when they were six weeks old, their clothes were shortened and they were christened, as I was. The Methodist minister came to the house to christen me.

My father was a master baker who went to sea. He sailed out of Liverpool and spent a lot of time away but never forgot to send postcards home, which I still have. Mother had been a dressmaker and served seven years apprenticeship at a big shop in Maryport. From the shop, apprentices were sent out in the morning to the big houses to do sewing for the day.

I was the middle child of a family of four daughters and one son. All of us children were given family names and I had to be called after Grandma. So I was christened Sarah Ann, which I hated, but right from the beginning I was always called Annie. We lived with my grandmother and my mother's only sister, Auntie Molly. Auntie Molly was the Headmistress of Broughton Moor School and also went about giving talks to the Methodists.

My earliest memory is of going to school at three years of age. That was usual in those days and my mother took me by the hand, up Church Street, leaving me at school. The rest of the time I had to find my own way there. There were three large schools in Maryport, the British School, the Catholic School and the National School, and I went to the National. This was a Church of England school but children from different denominations went there. A mixture of good, bad and in-different went to all three schools. The British School thought they were better than the National but we showed them the difference. We could always beat the 'British' at football and various games.

The National School went the whole length, from Eaglesfield Street to Fleming Street. Inside there was a section each for boys, girls and infants. Each room had a stove and there were times when the stoves got red hot and it was beautiful and warm. Outside we had a school yard where we played. We started off using a slate and on Fridays the pupil who had worked hardest came round and collected the slates. The teachers were strict but kind. Before I started school Mr Bailey had been Headmaster. He was followed by Mr Walter who was already a teacher there and made a lovely Headmaster.

School started at nine a.m. until twelve. Then we had until half-past one to eat and were at school until four o'clock. There was over forty pupils in each class and over 600 children in school. Dunces were in one division and bright ones in another. We learned how to spell and do our tables, which was a lot of reciting in those days ('one two is two, two twos are four').

On our school outings we didn't go very far, just to Bassenthwaite or Keswick, places like that. We travelled by Scott's horse-drawn wagonettes from Ellenborough, carrying our mugs and food. We usually went to Isel Hall for our tea, which we had in the stables. On the way to Isel Hall there was one part where we all had to get out of the wagonette and push it up the hill.

In those days Maryport was very important, especially with the sailor boys. But there were times when the sailor boys were out of work for at least six months and their boats were laid up. When this happened they sometimes received money from the parish, as there was no dole. Now my grandma was boss of our house and if she heard of one of her grandchildren going near the Parish Rooms she was very, very angry. Once, when Auntie Molly was little, she'd gone with a little pal to the Post Office. When Grandma asked her where she'd been, Auntie Molly said, 'Oh, where they're giving money out.' What a dressing down she got, because Grandma thought she'd been to the Parish Rooms.

There was a lot of poverty, and schoolchildren who couldn't afford dinner went to the Coffee Tavern in Senhouse Street for free school meals. But there was also the better off. Some were sea captains but others were just ordinary sailor boys and miners.

At home we all had our jobs to do. Friday was market day, when the ladies all dressed up and went to market, up in the Market Square [Fleming Square]. The square is still there but not the market. It was a wonderful place and as schoolchildren we were allowed out of school half an hour early at 11.30 to spend our Friday's penny. That was all we had for the week. One stall sold mint balls and toffee which we were

Market Place (now Fleming Square), Maryport

Shipping Brow, Maryport

allowed to take back to school in the afternoon and it was looked after until hometime.

They were great believers, in those days, in providing good food. Oatmeal porridge was made the night before in a big pan and then it was heated up in the morning and we'd have a lovely basin of porridge before we went to school. When we came home from school we had a good dinner, not a sloppy meal like they have today. And if you didn't like it, you didn't get anything else.

Potato Hash was a great favourite in our family. Oh, I hated it but I had to eat it. And Potato Pot was another regular item. We always said 'potato', never 'tatie'. You see, with Auntie Molly being a teacher, we learnt to speak properly. Teatime was another proper meal and for supper we had a piece of bread with sugar on it and a drink of milk. Granny was a great believer in milk.

Every week my mother and Granny had a baking day when they baked their own bread and teacakes. People helped each other and so many of the teacakes and loaves were given out to neighbours or friends. My mother used to bake a lovely round cake. I can see it now. It was always round, baked in the oven, then sliced and buttered. Lovely.

I always remember there was a butcher's shop in Maryport and it was kept by two ladies. At Christmas there was the most wonderful toy in the window. It was a little clockwork mouse that crept up to a mousetrap and, just as it was going to be beheaded, it ran back. That toy was in the butcher's window every Christmas for years. When the two ladies died, I was grown up and tried to find out about the toy but never managed to. People didn't have Christmas trees then; they had a Kissing Bush which hung from the ceiling in the living-room. It was made of holly and had all sorts of little toys on it and was kept up until New Year when the children got the toys. We always had full stockings on Christmas Day, with a sixpenny piece, sweets and small things like that. Then we went to church, you bet we did. But someone stayed at home to make the dinner. This was usually chicken and Christmas pudding, which I didn't like.

I was a naughty little girl. I used to go off with other boys and girls to play when I wasn't supposed to. Not far, mind you. We used to play marbles, bouncing balls and skipping on the street but there was plenty of room and time in those days. We weren't supposed to go near the harbour, being well brought up. Even for playing out I never wore clogs, never. I always wore shoes and rarely put a pinafore over my dress.

I can't say I remember a great deal about the First World War. I know I used to run errands for the people in the area. It was always 'Annie will do it'. At school we carried on as normal, but outside school anything that was eatable we had to queue for, waiting our turn for such as margarine when we'd been used to fresh butter.

Many years ago there was only two political parties, the Liberals and the Conservatives. My father was a great Liberal, but as the years passed most of the family changed to Conservative. Polling day was funny. Women from 'down street' would nearly have fought for the party they supported. Then Labour came into fashion and a lot of people changed over to that. They dressed in red or had red trimmings on their hats to go and vote. Polling day isn't like it used to be. People go and give their vote and that's all there is to it.

I was fourteen years of age when I went to Thomlinson Girls School at Wigton. My parents had to pay and it was £10 a quarter which was a lot of money. Our winter uniform was a navy blue pinafore dress with a white blouse and in summer we wore a green linen pinafore instead. We had to wear a straw boater with a band of ribbon in the school colours round it and were known as 'Miss Wildman's young ladies'.

Miss Wildman was the Headmistress and she once caught me reading one of Ethel M. Dell's books. You see, I'd hidden this book and brought it out at playtime, thinking the Headmistress wouldn't see it. That playtime it rained and we got into a little group and there I was, reading Ethel M. Dell to the girls, when the Headmistress came in and caught us. I got quite a telling off, as leader of the group. She sent for me and oh, she was angry. I had not to read such a trash.

About six of us who went home from school by train walked through Wigton to the railway station and passed a shop that made ice-cream.

One day, as we had plenty of time for the train and Miss Wildman was nowhere about, we went into the shop. Out we came with cornets, when a bus stopped right at the door of the shop and Miss Wildman was on the bus. Nothing was said then but the next morning at school all six of us had to go up on the stage in front of everybody. For the rest of the term we had to have prayers with the kindergarten and weren't allowed to take part in Speech Day. Our parents were there but we had to sit with the little ones.

Normally children left school at fourteen and the girls went away into service and the boys went to the pits or on to ships. There wasn't a matriculation exam in those days but at Wigton School we had to sit a very hard exam which consisted of ten subjects (even sewing was included). I passed this exam and returned to the National School to be a pupil teacher until I trained to be a qualified teacher. My wage was paid monthly and was very, very little in those days. My mother took charge of the money and gave me some back.

I also had to do a correspondence course, which wasn't easy. The papers went away every week to be marked and, I must say, I got very good marks. All the pupil teachers had to sit the final exam at school on a day when the children had a holiday. We sat the exam while teachers walked up and down the corridors and watched as we did the written work. When I passed the exam I stayed at the National School.

I taught the nine- and ten-year-olds and the class was very, very big. Each class was still divided into two, with the bright children in the upper division and the other children in the lower division. We managed very well indeed because of the large rooms. For religious instruction we joined up with another class, so you can imagine what a big class it was, with eighty children, but there was always good behaviour, always. For really hard discipline we went to the Headmaster with the offender, but for ordinary discipline we just landed them one. We didn't have much trouble, as the parents always backed us up.

Truancy was very frequent with the boys in those days but the School Board Man brought them back to school and the boys had to behave. Girls always stayed away from school on wash day and looked after the baby or smaller children, always. You see, the majority of mothers had such large families in those days. The fathers were usually away at sea and the mother was up at five o'clock in the morning to do the washing. And she used to do it all in a day. Women had hard lives, spending their days working and looking after children.

Every house had a set pot for the washing. It was made of iron and oh, the water used to bubble and boil. All the whites were washed first and as far as I can remember only soda was added to the water but everything came out beautiful. The set pot was a fixture in every cellar on our street and Monday was usually wash day.

Measles was rife in those days but consumption was the worst, absolutely the worst. So many of the poorer children had it. Little ones died of it and the older ones stayed off school and went so thin as if they hadn't had much to eat. Oh, it was terrible but gradually consumption died out. Of course clinics were opened and the children attended these weekly to be examined. You never hear of that illness now and children at school are very, very healthy.

When I started teaching, children still left school at fourteen unless they won a scholarship. Youngsters who didn't pass the scholarship and had brains could work their way up and get good jobs. Those that won a scholarship left the junior school at eleven years of age and went to the secondary school at Workington. The ones that left school at fourteen still went into service or to the pits. There was a lot of pits in the area in those days. Very early in the morning a man went round the streets shouting what time it was. Then, shortly after, the train went along to Siddick pit taking the miners to work. Of course there were accidents at the pits and the miners would be taken to Grasslot Hospital. We still have the hospital but it's for older people now.

I had a good social life. I played tennis down at the posh place, Nether Hall, and hockey for the school and Maryport. Then netball came into fashion and we played that. I'd started courting and had lots of boyfriends. When I was courting (this would be when I was eighteen) I had to be home for nine o'clock. If not, Auntie Molly was there behind the front door and it was 'paddy whack' for me. In the end I used to leave the boy at the bottom of the street instead of him coming to the house with me. I had offers of marriage but I preferred to remain single and have a good time.

Maryport was one of the first places in the area to have a carnival. It really started 'down street' long before the Second World War. One of the mothers was marvellous at teaching dancing and a troupe of girls did a wonderful dance round the streets in the procession. For a long time there was no carnival and then it was revived and grew bigger and bigger until the town joined in. Now it's a noted carnival that comprises all Maryport and district.

During the 1920s and '30s there was a lot of poverty and hardship due to the Depression. I was one of the lucky ones who was working, teaching at the National School. Children still went to the Coffee Tavern for free meals and the adults went to Johnny Rafferty's. He was a character, working his way up and eventually becoming a town councillor. Johnny looked after the poor and gave them their meals – he was really a very, very good man. Our Methodist minister became great friends with him and they worked together. Maryport had a lot of characters in those days. I like Maryport. The people are homely, they're not stuck up. Oh, I like the town very much indeed.

With the Second World War, there was lots of rationing again and queuing for food but we wanted for nothing and were really well off. In the evenings the blinds came down and you had to find your way home in the darkness but you never heard any grumbling. I used to find my way home by feeling along the windowsills in John Street until I knew it was my house.

Late one Saturday night or early Sunday morning we heard a noise and of course everybody got up. We had a large tree growing at the back of our house and this aeroplane flew right over very, very slowly as though it was hunting for something. Then it dropped the bombs. Seven people were killed and four were from one house. This house belonged to the Howards, who were shopkeepers. The Howards had a school-teacher staying with them and she thought Maryport was a lovely place, with no war, no trouble of any kind. So her mother came to stay with her and had only just arrived on the twenty minutes to five train from Carlisle. They made their way to the Howards, had their tea and finally went to bed. The teacher, her mother and Mr and Mrs Howard were killed outright. We never, never expected Maryport of all places to be bombed. It was always the most peaceful, quiet little town.

I had an uncle, a retired naval officer, who lived two doors from us. Every night he came to our house and waited until he heard the nine o'clock news on the wireless, then he said 'Good night' and off he went. He never heard the bombing. Although we banged and knocked on his door, it didn't wake him. The next morning he wanted to know what all the fuss was about.

The British School was also bombed – it was absolutely wiped off the face of the earth – and the pupils came to the National School. We then had what was called 'Half Time' teaching. Our own pupils at the National School were taught in the mornings and the British School pupils were taught by their own teachers in the afternoons. After three months we changed around. We taught in the afternoons and 'British' pupils attended in the mornings.

About this time, I organised 'Physical Exercises' for the old ladies over sixty and it was great. A friend tootled on the piano while I took the ladies for drill and they did enjoy it. We wore nice green woolly outfits with short skirts that showed those wobbly legs. Oh yes, we had great fun. And when Prince George, the Duke of Kent, visited Maryport he came 'down street' to watch us all doing drill.

We had evacuees in Maryport who attended school. I remember a Jewish boy from Newcastle whose grandfather was a rabbi. When we were having religious instruction he listened to the Old Testament but sat on his own at the other end of the room reading when I taught about the New Testament. Do you know, when we had an examination that boy sat with the other children and he knew every answer. He'd been listening all the time about the New Testament, when he shouldn't have been. He was a lovely boy and I've often wondered what happened to him after he left.

After school hours I helped to put on shows that the children took part in and we made money for the soldiers and lots of charities. We even gave money to St Dunstan's (for the disabled servicemen) and they were thrilled to bits, showing us all around. Maryport people are resilient and when I put the children's concerts on during the war, they came in the blackouts and it didn't bother them. To celebrate the end of the war, we each took some food to school and had a party. We also had parties in the streets and set out tables the length of the streets. Oh, it was lovely.

After the war, we went on our merry way and in 1950 our school became the Maryport Church of England Camp Street School. We still had discipline but over the years that has gone in schools and the children certainly do miss it. The upper and lower divisions in classes was done away with in schools, so there was just one stream. I don't know what happens now but we taught all the children to read and write. Of course there were children who couldn't do certain things and would never be

Maryport Church of England School, 1961 (Annie is on the far left)

able to, but we didn't let them slip through our fingers. We had to teach them to read and write, we didn't wait until they were ready. We believed in getting on with the job. Mind, this is a long time ago.

It was while I was teaching that I was approached to be a magistrate. At first I refused but I was persuaded. I remember I had to go in front of a gentleman at Carlisle who asked all sorts of questions before I was made a magistrate and then every third Friday I had to attend court. For a long time I was a magistrate and then it was decided that I should be the Head of the Maryport bench. I held this position until I retired. Usually it was the menfolk who appeared in front of the Bench, mostly for fighting or occasionally for stealing. None of them bore me any illwill at all, and although it's many years ago now some of the men still speak to me and say 'How Do'. One of these men was an absolute devil until he became a grandfather and it changed his life. He took that baby everywhere with him and whenever I see him he still gives me a wave.

I always was one for writing letters and I loved 'composition' as we called it at school. And as for writing books, I simply loved it. I wrote about Maryport because I belong here and know all about the shipping. I asked people questions and used to find out all sorts of things. Until recently I used to go into school and teach the children about ship-building in Maryport. I used to give one or two of my books to the child who wrote the best composition. My books were sent all over the world and I received letters which said 'Thank you very much'. These were from people who had lived here, or else their mothers and fathers were from Maryport. You see, quite a lot of people emigrated, especially during times of unemployment. They went mostly to America, Canada or Australia. Their descendants still live there but they often come to Maryport for their holidays. They think there's no place on earth like Maryport.

In 1960 I received the MBE for public services, which was a surprise. This wonderful letter came from the Queen – I thought it was marvellous. I went to Buckingham Palace with my youngest sister, as she was teaching in London, and one of my good friends whose husband was lost in the war. As visitors they sat in a big hall, while up in the balcony the band played such lovely tunes. People who were receiving medals went into another room and I won't tell you how many times we visited the toilets, with the long wait and excitement.

Unfortunately the Queen was in Africa but the Queen Mother presented the medals and she was absolutely lovely. I remember when they called my name and I had to march into the room. Inwardly I was nervous. Finally I came and stood in front of the platform where the Queen Mother and certain gentlemen were. I went up the steps and curtsied four times to her and she presented me with my medal. She pinned it on me, gave me the box for it, shook hands and I curtsied again before marching off. I was taken to a room, where my medal was unpinned and put in a box, then it was down to the room where the presentation was being held to watch the others. At the end of the ceremony we were allowed to shake hands and speak to each other. There was one gentleman and I thought, 'Ee, I know you, I wonder who you are?' And he was a Maryport boy and I did know him. Talk about rejoicing.

I wasn't quite sixty when I retired from school. The school curriculums were changing and I was delighted to leave, as a lot of teachers were. What did I do then? What did I not do? I did all the things that I wanted to do, I did them all. I travelled. Shall I tell you where? Right. Different parts of England, France, Germany, Luxemburg, Ireland, Greece and Russia. So many places I can't remember. We cruised to the Holy Land which was beautiful and I spent three Christmases on board ship.

One Christmas the ship I was on was sailing down the waters off West Africa. Dinner was over and the guests and crew were taking their seats in preparation for the children's play, *The First Christmas*. Soon all was ready: the orchestra, guests and children, 2,000 in all. The lights

Annie at Maryport Harbour, 1980s

were dimmed, the orchestra was quietly playing Christmas music and the children were ready to take their turns. There were tears in many of the watchers' eyes. Eventually the play was over and, as one American lady said, 'The children have put Christmas aboard the ship.' I often think of that night and wonder where the children are, now grown up, in all parts of the world. Perhaps some are dead, some are married, but I hope that many of them give a thought to that wonderful night so long ago. I still have a photograph of the children to remind me of *The First Christmas*.

By this time Auntie Molly and my parents were dead. I was living alone but I had all my friends and was never lonely. Now the place where I'm living for elderly people, I opened it. The gentleman who owns it, I taught him as a little boy. He was a naughty little boy but he's grown into a wonderful person. I've always been interested in people. It's how I was born, I was always full of life. Granted, upbringing helps, if it's done properly. I've always helped with charity work and been invited to the garden parties at Buckingham Palace on various occasions. Then I helped with Cumbria's Silver Jubilee Appeal and met the Prince of Wales at Greystoke Castle.

Years and years ago, Maryport was a great ship-building port but that's all gone. There's so much unemployment now and very, very few fishing boats. At the present time men are working hard rebuilding the docks and all we hope now is that there is plenty of trade. But whatever has happened to Maryport, the people have stuck together. They are a wonderful set of people. I would never leave, I'm part of Maryport.

FIFTEEN

'*I used to say I'd never live on a farm . . .*'

ANN ROUTLEDGE (b. 1899)
Flimby/Glenridding/Martindale

'**C**um and sit on t'stool and Ah'll hod thu, than thoo'll git acquentid wid t'coo.' That's what my uncle at Flimby Hall Farm used to say to me when he was milking. I hated farming, I hated the smell. I used to say I'd never live on a farm or marry a farmer.

My mother was from farming stock but my father was a miner at Watergate pit, or 'Waattery Yat' as he used to call it. I can remember strutting around with Dad's tin bottle and pretending I was going to work. The bait box and bottle were both tin because there were so many mice down the pit. I've heard my father say that you hadn't to sit a minute before all these mice were round your feet, picking at the crumbs. Aye, there was quite a lot of pits and they say it's a trelliswork of mines under the sea.

I was born in 1899 at Flimby, which is just a mile from Maryport and four miles from Workington. We lived in a three-bedroomed house because we were a mixed family – four sons, three daughters and Granda. Granda was a real oldtimer and never off the shore. He used to keep us going with coal, bagloads of it. Then my mother had to get my uncle at the farm to go and collect all these bags of coal and bring them home. Granda had been a miner (it was in the family was mining). You couldn't turn them away from it; mining was all they talked about.

All my brothers went into the pits. We had two tin baths for when they all came home. The set pot was on all day for hot water, a great big fire banked up to the chimney and towels galore. We were lucky as none of my brothers had an accident but my father's brother was killed in a gas explosion – him and another three. Being an underground boss, Dad was allowed so many bags of coal but my brothers didn't get any. When a strike was on, a big opencast place was opened above Flimby and you could take bags and get coal from there. I know when the miners were on strike, with being a close community, each day one woman in the street would make a meal in a huge set pot. Everybody put vegetables or whatever they had into this set pot and shared the meal. Then the next day it would be someone else's turn.

My youngest brother Tom was so delicate, and a bit brainier than the other lads, so Mother got him another job. But he didn't like the job and drifted back to the mines. Mother was broken-hearted and said, 'Fancy, A've saved und scraped tu keep 'im out' t' pits.' 'Well, Mother,' I answered, 'the urge is there, you can't stop it.' He was a grand lad was my youngest brother and got to be a Labour Representative for the miners when he was nineteen and went to London for a conference. My mother cried for days, she thought she would never see Tom again.

He was a good talker and he enjoyed the meetings. It was a rough job for him to take on at that age, he was too young. People used to call him Gentleman Tom but he didn't care, he only laughed at them. Politics was taken very seriously in those days. There used to be fights among the Liberal and Labour supporters. Women used to dye their sheets red or blue and hang them out of the window or on the clothes lines. Everybody wore big rosettes and I can remember making mine.

Ann's youngest brother, Tom

We all helped each other in them days. Father used to say to me, 'Gar und see waat pinny yeer muther's taakun wid 'er.' You see, she was the midwife and layer-out, so she had a black pinny if anybody was going to die and a white one for the new babies. She had these pinnys ready, as folk used to come all times of day and night for her. I've seen her dragging covers off the bed.

163

'Waat's tu taakun noo, Muther?' my father would say.

'Well, the poor sowl's cauld, she hes nee mair cliaas, Ah'll hev tu waarm 'ur up. Ah'll fetch it back.'

The covers never came back though.

Oh, it was a big occasion when a baby was born. They used to make a big bowl of rum butter. Rum butter on crackers, I used to love them. I remember one of my sisters meeting Dad coming from work and him saying, 'And waat's Muther been diunn'?'

'Oh, she's med a tatie-pot for yu und she's maackun sum rum butta. Are wi ganna hev a babby?'

Dad was mad and Mother says to my sister, 'Ah'll put a tac [clip] in ayther side uf thee mooth, it's ower big.'

I'll tell you something I've never seen anybody else do. When Mam made broth with a sheep's head and lump of bacon, she'd peel potatoes and wrap them in a towel. The towel was fastened at each end and put in. Then when it was taken out, the potatoes had such a lovely flavour.

When people died, there was funeral biscuits to eat. These were special teacakes with lots of fat in them. They were lovely to eat without butter. If folk had any money they bought ham and made ham sandwiches with these buns, which were better still. There was always plenty of drink at funerals. Wherever it all came from, I'll never know.

I wasn't quite four when I started at Flimby School and it was awful. Outside there were four toilets next to each other, with little holes in the side. Boys used to take a stick into the toilets with them and shove it through, prodding whoever was in the next loo. It was a mixed class when you started, but when you were about five you were split up. The infants school was pandemonium. We played more than anything, it wasn't organised. Then, as we moved up to other classes, we had sums, reading, scripture and, really, there was very little variety. The classes were big because every family had at least six or seven children in those days. My mother was very friendly with a Mrs Twentyman who had twelve children, so no wonder my mother was a good friend to her.

I loved the shore and was never off it. Buckets full of cuvvins [winkles] I've gathered, just like snot. And Mother would chase us with them. She used to say they were sea snails. Going round the docks at Maryport was a treat. When my brothers had a day off work, they'd take me there. You could see all the big ships, the sailors sitting smoking and the fishing boats coming in. There was a noted pub down there that my elder brothers used to go to and stop until morning.

You see, sailors got their wages when they docked. There was plenty of drink, and women (or 'dock wallopers' as they were called) would be there. Nobody had to let on they'd been at that pub.

I remember one brother saying to another, 'Ah know whear thoo waas.'

'Ah-wheel, dooant let Faather und Muther know' was the answer.

Oh, Christmas was great. Mother made me a bush, a whole lot of holly tied up, and hung it on the ceiling with all these lovely baubles. Our lads used to buy mistletoe and invite girls and have kissing competitions under these bushes. I'd never seen or heard tell of Christmas trees until lately, it was all these little bushes. I had a stocking for Christmas but there was never much put into it. Sometimes I got a sugar pig with a pink tail and I'd keep it until it was nearly black.

One year my brothers bought a gramophone with cylinders and I thought we were the cat's whiskers. All the neighbours used to come and stand in the yard and Mother would open the windows to let them listen. Mother had a favourite piece of music. She wasn't really religious but she was having a tough time with Father and when she heard:

> If I could only take your hand,
> As I did when I took your name,
> You're only a beautiful picture
> In a beautiful golden frame

she would sit down and weep. Of course, our lads were mad on music. There was a drum and fife band that one of them was in. Two were singers and in the choir and it was a very good men's choir at Flimby. So we always had a bit of music.

At New Year the ships blew their horns and church bells were ringing. It was lovely. 'Open arl t'dours t'let New Year in. Open all the winders as weel,' Mother used to say. Then it was 'Happy New Year' and the glasses and bottles would come out and neighbours would come in. Three fellows from Dad's work used to come and wait in the yard until it was midnight. They came in the house then and gave Mother this great big piece of coal but there had to be a glass of whisky for it.

'A dear bit of coal,' Mother would say.

Father always answered, 'It's un auld custum, we'll hev t'carry it on.'

Every spring we were given 'opening medicine'. Oh, it was awful. Mother used to put a little bit of syrup on the bottom of a spoon and castor oil on top of that. I'll tell you what was a good 'medicine' but it was too expensive. Granny used to soak big raisins in rum. Not these little ones but real big ones.

I said to Mother one day, 'I think I need some raisins.'

'Well,' she said, 'thoo'll hefta waant, becos thur isn't any in my hoose. Ah can't afford sek things. Besides it's nobbut two days sen thoo hed yaan.'

Grandma was my mother's mother and she was a real old worker. She did farm but when her husband died she bought this little house with a smallholding, just as you get to Siddick. The only trouble was that Grandma kept pigs and I used to say to my mother, 'I'll go and see Grandma but I'm not going to see them smelly pigs.'

'Thoo'll hev tu gaa and see them smelly pigs 'cos she leeves fur them pigs,' answered Mother.

Grandma worked till she dropped and that's the way to do. She lived till she was over ninety, so I'm keeping the tradition up.

I was only ten when my father died with cancer. I'll tell you what he thought caused it. My older brothers bought him this pipe, which was terribly posh. When Dad came home from work he used to sit smoking this pipe and wait to let the young ones get washed first. One day he went to sleep and this pipe stuck to his mouth with all the coal dust and dirt and had to be pulled off. Dad said the cancer started from there, in his face, and twisted itself right down his neck.

There was no treatment at all. There was no nurses either. You had to nurse your sick people at home yourself. My mother's hands were blue with Condis Fluid, as she had to wash every time she did anything for Dad. Dad wore a scarf over the bandages on his face when he used to take me to and from school. Here I was tripping away with him, to take his mind off his illness, and I felt so sorry for him. Men did more drinking then and we should have been well off but Dad spent money he shouldn't have. He saw his folly on his death bed, which was very hard lines. He used to say, 'Ah allus meant tu school thee, Ann. Ah wus ganna buy thu a piaana and git thu laarnt tu play.' Dad had been selfish but of course men were selfish then, they really were.

Poor old Mother, her back must have been broad. I wish she had lived a little bit longer so that I could have given her something back. When you're young you leave school and you're living your own life. I gave her all the money I could but that wasn't what I wanted. I wanted to love her and do things for her, which I could have in later years. Oh, she was a great mother.

It was sad when Edward [King Edward VII] died. I remember my mother dyeing an old clout black and hanging it out of the window on a pole. For King George and Queen Mary's Coronation, there was a big 'do' on at Maryport but I wasn't able to go because I had scarlet fever. I'd been on the shore and hanging over a dead dog that had been drowned, so whether I got some infection off it I don't know. I remember I was put into Mother's four-poster bed and I thought I was the Queen Bee in this blinking bed.

I left school when I was fourteen because I knew Mother was needing the money. Mrs Twentyman's daughter used to work at the Ullswater Hotel, so I thought, 'I'm going to see Beryl and ask her to get me a job.' Well, she got me a job at Ullswater and I've been here ever since. To get to Ullswater, one train a day travelled from Flimby to Troutbeck, near Penrith. We had to wait at Troutbeck Station and inside the waiting-room was a harmonium that anyone could play to pass the time away. I remember a girl called Mary Rose from Workington was also going to the hotel with me and she was playing this harmonium when the stationmaster came in. Showing off to us bits of kids, he said he would give us a song. He stood up to sing 'There'll always be an England', spread his chest out and burst the top brass button of his coat! You know at that age you'll giggle at owt, and we all started to laugh. He thought he was so superior.

At Troutbeck Station we had to wait until this horse-drawn coach met us and we went over Troutbeck Moor and along the lake edge. It was a long journey all the way to the Ullswater Hotel but the coaches made that journey every day. I thought the hotel was gorgeous.

Ullswater Hotel

I started work as pantry maid for ten bob a week, which I sent home to my mother. Later I trained as a waitress and got tips which I was able to keep. For the staff there were two double beds in a bedroom, which four shared. I shared a bed with one of the Twentyman girls. The 'Missus' used to knock us up about six o'clock in the morning but we'd sneak back to bed and she would come and waken us again. Then we

167

Ullswater Hotel staff, c. 1914 (Ann is in the back row, third from the right)

used to rush and make a cup of tea, as that was all we got until our breakfast at eight o'clock.

Quite a lot of West Cumberland girls worked at the hotel eventually. We recommended it to our friends, until there was thirteen of us Flimby girls working there. We wore cotton frocks and white aprons when we got up and everybody was allotted so much work. One person cleaned the sitting-room, another did the hall, another did the gentlemen's lavatories and so on. Then at nine o'clock, for serving breakfast, we changed into black with white cap and cuffs. I thought I was such a toff.

We finished work after nine o'clock at night, when we'd washed up after dinner. All the local lads used to come to the top gate near the hotel and you could pick yourself a man. All we did was walk through the woods, chat and have a singsong. We had to be back at the hotel by ten at night. You can laugh about it but a chap from the hotel used to come and ring a bell, shouting for us to return. That's how I met my husband – he was one of the local farm lads – and I'd always said I would never marry a farmer. I had one half-day off a week. Otherwise it was work and sleep but I was happy. I didn't manage to get home because it was such an effort to get to Troutbeck for the train. However my brothers used to come and see me when they could.

One place that we used to go to in our time off, was Charlie Dixon's. His photo is everywhere now, holding that sheep around his neck. Well, Charlie shared a cottage with his sister Grace at Hartsop, below the

Brotherswater Inn. It was a lovely old-fashioned cottage they had, full of old-fashioned things. They used to make us fresh eggs on toast, so it was a nice place to visit when the First World War was on. Charlie wasn't very tall, had long hair, and he was very dry spoken. He wouldn't work. He just kept a cow for their own use, a few chickens and the odd sheep. Someone would give him a pet lamb and he would bring it up, you see. Then he had a pony and trap that he used to collect branches for burning, as he never bought any coal.

The owners who ran the Ullswater were called Bowness and their family owned hotels at Windermere. They were brothers and were good to work for but strict. I remember when I was a waitress the owner's wife used to come and check our fingernails and make sure they were clean. You see, we used to get nobility as guests. Mr Bowness kept the hotel very select, he wouldn't let any trippers in. Most of the guests were lovely but you never got to know them because you only served them. Gorgeous meals we served, one course after another. I never knew you could get such food until I went there. We also got a lot of Newcastle businesspeople who were very wealthy and then, when the First World War was on, we got a lot of wounded soldiers.

With being colliers, my brothers were exempt from joining up but Ab, my husband-to-be, was in France. He got the Military Medal but he would never tell me why. 'Ah did nowt thut anybody else waadn't diuu.' That's all I got out of him. I know that one time Ab walked over Kirkstone Pass when he was coming home on leave. A blizzard was raging and he fell into a hole. He didn't know where he'd landed because it was all snowed up. Anyway he'd landed in the driver's seat of a coach but managed to struggle out and continue home. Coaches used to come over Kirkstone in the summertime but not in winter. So it must have been a freak snowstorm and the driver had got the horses loose, taken them down into Patterdale and left the coach up on Kirkstone.

I was twenty-one when I got married at Flimby. I remember the first thing my husband said when we came out of the church: 'Whoa's that hoss in t'field?' That's how much of the service he took in. There used to be three little cottages opposite the White Lion at Patterdale and we lived in one of those when we first married. The cottage had one room upstairs and one downstairs. There was no sink, tap or toilet and just a paraffin lamp. Both the toilet and sink were outside, along the hedge, by the side of the cottages. We had to take a bucket with us for the water and the slops we had to throw out. We did have an oven but it was hopeless, you could only make stews. Fortunately I was friendly with the owners of the White Lion and they let me use their oven at times. Oh, it was an awful life. You were working all day and had nothing to show for it.

Ab during the First World War

The White Lion was a homely place with beams and it was very dark. Fellas used to spend booze nights, Saturday nights, there. Mrs Sissons, the landlady, was a lovely person. Anybody in need and she was there to help. She would have a 'whip round'.

'Come on you lads, out with your pennies. So and so's poorly and he's got two children and not much money.'

Then all the men gave some money and that was a regular thing.

There used to be some jollification at the White Lion when the local hunt was there. Mrs Sissons would make some sandwiches and broth and there'd be a singsong. It was a lively concern. First one used to sing, then another. I know I said 'sing' but you wouldn't have liked to hear some of them, it was like dogs yowling. Old 'Hunty' Bowman was a character and he used to get drunk, start singing and blow his hunting horn. He nearly always got drunk and they had to take him home right over the fell. 'Hunty' had a song wrote about him, you know. Then there was Joe Weir and he was lively. He couldn't dance but used to pretend he could. Joe would put his cap on the floor and dance round it, singing hunting songs. They all liked their booze did them hunters.

Women didn't go in pubs in those days. Some relations came and lodged up at Hartsop and on this Saturday night they came to the pub and the wife was with her husband. I said to Ab, 'What's she come for?' Do you know, she stood outside that pub. She didn't go in, just stood there until he came out. It was a terrible thing if a woman went in a pub. It was 'Oh, his wife goes in pubs', you know. Women stayed at home and looked after their children.

At this time my husband was working in a quarry at the bottom of Kirkstone. It was a hard job because them stones took some handling. He used a horse and cart and the bottom of the cart was lined with tin so that the stones wouldn't damage the wood. My husband was very good with horses and people used to bring him all sorts of horses to cure of bad habits.

Ab used to take visitors up Helvellyn. Years earlier he used to help with sheep near there, so he knew the area. Then he started taking a few visitors up Helvellyn by pony to see the sunrise. He did it all off his own bat and people recommended him to their friends. Once thirteen of us went to see the sunrise and it was black dark, as we didn't set off until half-past eleven at night. We went up past the houses in the village as far as the lead mines and turned up on to the fell. When we saw the sunrise it was a marvellous sight. At first there was just a few rays. Then it started to spread in this half-moon shape and it was just like a big ball of fire. But coming down from Helvellyn was worse than going up. You had to have your wits about you coming down Striding Edge.

The lead mines had been there a long, long time and all the cottages were miners' houses. It was rather sad they closed the mines, as that was where a lot worked. A lot of the cottages are holiday homes now and used in summer, so if there's anything going on in the village in winter there's none of the occupants here to support it.

We were at the cottage when my husband got a farm at Sandwick near Martindale because he'd been used to farming. The first day at the farm I asked Ab where the toilet was and he went to look for it. The toilet was two big holes in the ground, it was filthy. 'Oh,' I said, 'I'm not having

The Kirkstone Inn

this, I'll clean it out.' I got some dipping buckets, put them in and they were emptied every day. Folk at Martindale thought I was mad. I didn't like Sandwick, it was too lonely for me. I missed working at the hotel and was terribly lonely. You see, I'd been the youngest of seven at home and had a busy life, so it was purgatory for me. I know when I first went to the farm I cried buckets. At night owls were hooting, foxes were shouting and bucks were roaring. There was a lot of deer at that time and at rutting time I was frightened out of my skin by the noise.

Our farm was up all these hairpin bends on the fells, four and a half miles from Pooley Bridge. We used a tilley lamp for light and had an oil stove for cooking. We'd both said we'd never borrow any money because there would be no chance of paying it back, so we used what little we had on the farm. You can smile now when you think about it but it's amazing what you'll do when you're in a tight corner.

All the farms round here are sheep farms, and when you took over a farm you had to take over the sheep that were born on the fell, at a price. So my husband bought some sheep, as he thought he could look after some of his own as well as the owner's. Then we had about seven milk cows, as you need that many before it starts to pay. We got some chickens and every year my husband was breaking in somebody's horse and that brought some extra money in.

I was terrified of the horses and I remember one year I was peeling taties near the kitchen window and saw this wheel go by. A nephew who was staying at the time came running in shouting, 'Auntie, come quickly,

Martindale

come quickly. The horse has tipped the cart over. It's took off and I don't know where it's gone.'

I thought, 'Oh Lord, now then, what am I going to find?' I went round the building, up the fell, and there was my husband sitting on the horse's head. Do you know what he said? 'Has't thou got a match?' He was going to light his pipe in that predicament. He was a brave man.

I never liked cows and I wasn't going to learn milking but I learned how to make butter. Classes were started at church and five of us went. I did enjoy the company and the lessons and learnt to 'knock up' butter. That helped because times were hard. (It cost only five bob to buy a lamb.) To sell the butter I had to take it to Glenridding but that meant walking to Pooley Bridge and then catching the bus to Penrith.

A friend at the bottom of the hill had a boat and he used to lend me it, so I rowed across the lake with my butter. Many a time I was nervous, as the weather got up rough and the wind comes both ways across the lake. I'd never been out in a boat because my mother wouldn't even let me go out on the Solway when I lived at home. I wouldn't have cared but the boat wasn't seaworthy either and had a crack in it. So I had to put some sheep's wool and tar into the crack and hope for the best.

The snow could be bad in winter and the sheep would be stuck up on the fell. I went with Ab a few times to look for them. He'd take a long stick, poking it in the snow near the walls. You see, sheep would go beside a wall to shelter and they could get air when they were buried there. Stone walls aren't cemented and there would be pockets of air for

173

the sheep to breathe and it kept them alive. It was pitiful to see them – they couldn't stand when you got the snow off them. Generally Ab came for them with a trailer or the sledge and he would put them in a box or tie them on. It's all open fell is this place, so it was usually the sledge that was used.

Once we were snowed in at Sandwick for about a week and lived on scones. We used to get a sack of flour once a month, so we still had flour but no yeast. Our nearest neighbours had five children and they were in the same situation as us. We managed to break the ice on the lake and launch the boat that had been drying out for the winter. One of the men rowed across the lake, caught the bus to Penrith and brought some yeast back. After that we were rather fortunate, as a postman who called said, 'If thoo waants any yist, just tell mu', and he would bring it for us.

If we had to walk to Pooley Bridge, I've seen my husband and me rushing down these hairpin bends to catch the bus and Parson Roberts would be waiting for us. He was awfully kind and would have a big cup of coffee for me and a glass of rum for my husband. Mind you, when we'd been to Penrith, all the shopping was to hump up that hill to get home. It was no picnic I can tell you.

I used to go to the services at the little church on the top of the hill at Howtown every Sunday. One Sunday morning, a relation of my husband's was having her baby christened but Ab wasn't at church as he was gathering the sheep. Have you ever heard them gathering the sheep? They're swearing away at the dogs. 'You lazy old b———' and all this. The church door was open because it was such a lovely day and, as Parson Roberts was christening the baby, we could hear Ab outside cursing blue.

When I came out of the service, Parson Roberts said, 'Tell Ab, I heard him saying his prayers.'

'I'll say some prayers when I get home to him,' I answered.

Parson Roberts was a Welshman and a lovely singer. He would come and see us through the week and if I wasn't in he'd leave two cigarettes on the mantelpiece, one for Ab and one for me. I didn't smoke but Parson Roberts used to try and get me to, offering me a cigarette and saying, 'If you don't smoke now, you will do.' With going to church on Sunday, I didn't make dinner that day. Sunday dinner was on a Saturday, then it was a 'warm up' on Sunday. You respect Sunday and it's a change not having to cook, isn't it?

As I didn't like farming, we furnished some of our rooms and I took visitors in and had campers. That was more in my line, as I couldn't see us making anything with just farming. We were existing, that was all. Oh, the visitors were lovely and I made some good friends. I did them well and they felt they were at home. They got fresh butter and cream and we always had plenty of chickens, so I could kill a hen when we were hard up. It was a nice life with the visitors, it was my cup of tea.

The campers had to be tough in those days. When they first started coming they used to have old bits of tarpaulin or mackintosh to lie on. I knew one fella who used his mother's tablecloth. You know, the stuff that's like oilcloth. It was about this time that we got a little car and that made things a lot easier. But it was an awful spot to drive to. Lots of visitors used to leave their cars at the bottom of the hill. They wouldn't attempt to drive up it.

We'd been at Sandwick about eight years when I got asthma and the doctor told Ab it wasn't a proper place for me, so we moved. My husband had a brother who farmed at Patterdale and we stayed there, as it was a big house. When the Second World War came, we lived with a niece at Ambleside and did war work. Ab was on the ash cart, which he didn't like, with being used to country life. He used to say, 'Yu can't spit ower yur own doorer-step but wat sumboddy sees yu.' I got myself a job as a waitress at the Langdale Chase Hotel and I enjoyed that, as it's a beautiful place. We were kept busy, as a lot of south country people came to Ambleside and this area. They thought they'd be safer here, which they were.

As soon as the war was over, we came back to the farm at Patterdale, as Ab's brother had retired. We still took in visitors and campers but you never charged people for camping. They might give you something, but that was all. We were past retirement age when we left there. The cottage we moved to had no toilet. That was across the road and we had to bath by degrees. Tops and bottoms, that's the only way we could bath and I didn't like that. We weren't there long. I don't miss West Cumberland, as most that I knew there are dead and gone. I'll call and see relatives but I'm always pleased to come back here, this is my home. You see, Ab and me we were close all our life, we were a happy couple. I didn't like farming, so he had to tempt me with something, like a day off. We worked together, we did things together, we were happy.

SIXTEEN

'We both worked at Elsie's

✌

NORAH (b. 1919) & KATHLEEN (b. 1918)
Cockermouth

NORAH: I was the youngest in the family, born in 1919. My mother had eleven children altogether but four died, leaving five sons and two daughters. We lived at the bottom house in Lindsay's Yard, off the Main Street at Cockermouth. Our cottage had one room downstairs and two bedrooms. The tap was halfway up the yard and you just had a dish for water and got washed in the pantry. At weekends Mam got the bath out that used to hang behind the stairs door and we got bathed in front of the fire. The communal wash-house with the set pot was also in the yard. Everybody had their day for using the wash-house and for spring-cleaning; they all took their washing up to Fairfield. That's used as a car park now but then it belonged to the town. It was quite a bit from where we lived but people used to take their blankets to dry or stair carpets to beat. That's if you had carpets. Many folk didn't even have oilcloth, it was just bare flags.

Mam cooked over the fire for frying and at the side was a little black oven for baking. On Sunday mornings my dad would fry everybody's breakfast, using this big frying pan, and the food would go into the oven to keep warm until everybody was ready for their breakfast. You nearly always knew what meals you were going to have because they had to be prepared. Maybe on washing day it was potato hash, then the next day it would be broth.

Dad was a self-employed builder and used two old cottages as warehouses, which he paid one shilling and sixpence a week to rent. By the time I was born, three of my brothers were in the business with Dad and they did most of their work in the country – Lorton, Loweswater or Buttermere way. In the early days they would walk to where they were working but later on they biked. After that they got motorbikes.

KATHLEEN: I've known Norah most of my life. In all the years up until 1938 there was very little work to be had. Dad might get a job with the County Council when they were tar-spraying but as soon as that was finished he was laid off. It wasn't easy for my mother. She took in washing and you got sick to death of washing hanging over your head. You see, we did everything in the one downstairs room – eat, cook and sit. I remember one couple that my mother used to wash for. They had two lodgers and their washing was included. One of my brothers and me used to go on a Monday morning and collect this washing in a clothes basket. It got so heavy my father made us a wheelbarrow to go for it. All the washing was washed, dried, ironed and aired for two shillings and sixpence and I wouldn't be able to tell you how many times she said: 'Tell your mother I'll pay her next week.' Now this woman's husband was working and besides that he had two part-time jobs. They had the two lodgers and the woman worked at nights.

We started at Fairfield School when we were five. You went into the Infants first and there was Miss Mirehouse, Miss Wilson and Miss Tinker and the Headmistress was Miss Hodgson. You went through four classes in the Infants before going into the big school. I often used to get the cane, never for anything bad, just mischievous things like talking in class. But I would never have gone home and told my parents because I knew they'd have said, 'It's too bad she didn't give you twice as much.' Oh no, they were all in agreement to being punished at school. They would never have questioned the teacher, no such thing.

NORAH: I remember we had a good netball team at Fairfield. I was in Miss Peel's class for a long time. She was very keen on Shakespeare and we acted a lot of his plays. To help decorate the scenery for these plays, we used to go to Oakhurst Woods to pick laurel and greenery. Then we'd take old wooden clothes maidens to school and decorate them with the greenery for the background.

The good netball team at Fairfield School, 1930s
(Norah is standing far right, holding the ball)

We went to the Congregational Sunday School and there used to be 'Catch Me Pal' [a religious meeting] on Bridge Street. Those were little concerts they used to put on and give you little religious tracts and pictures. Basically we went to the Congregational Chapel because it was near where we lived.

In Cockermouth there was a nice covered market in the Market Place. There was stalls and country people used to come and you could buy their fresh butter, eggs, potatoes and soft fruit when it was in season. Palmers fish shop had a corner booth there for years, where you could buy fresh fish. Walter Willson's had a stand as well and Keenan's were there with their pots and pans. Old Mr Keenan had a pot shop at Gallowbarrow and came round with a horse and cart selling pots on a Saturday afternoon.

KATHLEEN: The hirings were held in the Market Place, with all the farmers and anybody who was for hire, on Fair Monday. A lot of farm lads would have put their six months in and their poor mothers would be waiting for them coming home with their money but by the time they came from the pub there'd be nothing left. Other lads had borrowed on their wages and had no money to bring home. If you went out on that day, some old farmer would ask, 'Is't thou for hire?' When somebody was hired, they were given a pound and that was their bond. They didn't break their word in them days. We also had the Irish drovers with their cattle come to the auction. They'd come in to Silloth by boat and get the train to Cockermouth.

NORAH: The shops were open much longer then. I used to go with my mam and dad on Saturday nights to Bewley's, the grocer's on Station Road, at about nine o'clock at night. Dad would buy us a hand of bananas and a few pounds of apples. That was our treat for the week. Old Johnny Hodgson stood on the street and Dad would buy twenty Gold Flake cigarettes and a quarter of toffees from him. Johnny grew vegetables and used to come into town on Saturday night with a big wheelbarrow with a canvas top, lit with big flares, and stand next door to the Globe on Main Street. When Mam and I went home, Dad would finish off in Jimmy Dixon's (that was the Spirit Vaults, next to the Globe). There was a lot of pubs in those days and Jennings have been here as long as I can remember. When they're brewing, you can smell that lovely smell on a fine day. We often used to go round and play near there.

KATHLEEN: My father, two brothers and me all had Sunday paper routes. Father had his paper bag at the end of Station Street and had

Beer being loaded up from Jennings Brewery in Cockermouth

customers there who came for their paper. Us kids had our rounds and customers and were often told, 'Come back next week and we'll pay you then' but quite a few didn't pay. The Sunday papers were sold for tuppence and we made a ha'penny on each one. So if somebody didn't pay for one you were really selling four papers for nothing. My brothers sold the *Lancashire Post* and they were on the street with that until the second house pictures came out.

NORAH: Summer we spent down at Beckside, that's where everybody played. The river has kind of changed its course now but then it used to nearly dry up and we could wade to the Mill Fields and go across to the Ladyboat. The Ladyboat was where the Derwent had a sluice and a fish trap. The big lads had a diving board there and on one side the Castle Field kids would play and on the other side was St Helen's Street kids.

If you went further up, through the woods, that took you up to Mickle Brow and at the right time of year you went for primroses and to pinch a few daffodils. Mickle Brow was kind of hilly and that's where we used to roll our pasche eggs. The place to go for white violets was Mill Lonnings and we always collected palm, pussy willow. It looks nice with daffodils and a bit of redcurrant, I can never resist picking it.

For Easter we had a new outfit and usually a new straw hat. Everybody went to Annie Scott's on Cocker Bridge, just below the castle, for their hats. The Scotts were an old Cockermouth family and Annie had the hat shop for a long, long time. She sold children's things and when you went up the stairs I think it was the Percy coat of arms on the wall. It was a very, very old property and belonged to the castle.

KATHLEEN: There was a lot of land attached to the castle then and Lord Leconfield used to come and stay there. You always knew when the old lord was in residence, as the flag was flying. He didn't live there permanently, just for a few weeks in the summer to do a bit of salmon fishing.

NORAH: Folk round here liked fishing. Everybody used to go round the Beckside at a certain time of the year because you could literally see dozens of salmon fins out of the water. Most people had salmon for tea and you didn't ask questions if anybody gave you a piece. In summer when we used to go across to the Mill Field there was the Mill Raise. It's all been filled in now but then it was quite deep and every summer the water was let out, so it could be cleared of weeds. Well, of course there was very often nice little trout that were trapped in the small amount of water that was left. For those few days, all the kids were there with snipers. These were made out of bed lats [wooden slats from beds] and were used to bat the fish and kill them. They got loads of fish that way.

There was an awful lot of TB in those days but you didn't hear of too many cases in Cockermouth. The patients went up to the sanatorium at Threlkeld and buses used to run on a Sunday up to the 'San'. I had an old auntie who lived in the Market Place and people used to take money to her every Friday night. This would be for the doctor's club and people paid a penny a week in case they needed the doctor. There was also the blanket club and by paying so much a week you got a couple of blankets. People also ran clog and stocking funds, which were similar.

KATHLEEN: I remember on Waterloo Street, when old people were very ill or dying, sawdust and straw was spread on the street so that the noise of horses and carts didn't disturb them. Up at Gallow-barrow was the Workhouse but that's gone now and also the Lodging House where vagrants and tramps would get shelter. We used to pass the Workhouse going to school and see the women in the kitchen kneading bread. In another part of the building was the laundry where we saw the women scrubbing clothes and outside were the men breaking stones for the roads.

There was two lots of vagrants that I remember. First there was the 'Meths Folk'. They were an old couple who used to show up once in a while and you could tell what they drank because their faces were purple. They couldn't go in any chemist's, as they wouldn't be served. What they did was get kids to go in the chemist's for them and get a big bottle of methylated spirits. Once they'd had that, the pair of them would argue, fight and shout at each other until the old lady would pass out. Her husband would bundle her into the old pram they had and push her back to where they were living rough.

The 'Bisto Kids' were similar but I don't think they were into booze. They used to show up every once in a while with their old pram that they kept everything in. I think they lived rough up on the Embleton Road while they were in the area, then they'd be gone for weeks and weeks. When they turned up, folk would say, 'The Bisto Kids are back'.

A knife-sharpener sometimes came round and the Rag Man who handed you a balloon if you had any rags. Then there was Paddy Kelly who kept the Bluebell pub on the Main Street. Kids used to go to him with rabbit skins and get a ha'penny or penny for them, depending on the quality. When the gypsies came, they camped up at the top of Embleton Road or brought the caravans into town and parked at Fairfield. We were always scared of them and never went near because folk used to say, 'They'll run away with you.'

NORAH: I was twelve when we moved further up the street, as Dad bought another house. It was quite nice and a bit bigger. We had a bathroom and a toilet inside, a wash house of our own and a little bit of front garden. Of course we needed more room because we were a big family. By this time one of my brothers was staying somewhere else because we were pushed for room. My grandma lived along the street and we could go and stay with her.

I left school at fourteen. That was the leaving age, unless you went on to the Grammar School. I fancied being a hairdresser and my dad made enquiries about it. But in those days you had to pay to train and I was going to have to go to Carlisle and stay there, so that was the end of hairdressing.

I went to work at my sister's confectioner's shop, Elsie's, on the Main Street and was quite happy to go there. Because she was my sister, I think she was lenient with me. I never got a wage, she just bought me clothes and kept me. She said that she got very little in her youth, as there wasn't a lot of money to spare, and she bought me things that she would have liked. So really, in a way I was lucky.

KATHLEEN: We both worked at Elsie's. I started there at fourteen and served my time. For half a crown a week, I started work at seven in the morning and never got home much before half-past five at night. The first job was to put the fire on and get the oven going. We set the fire off with coals and sticks, then chopped coke up and stoked the fire up with the coke. We always threw a spot of water on with the coke. I don't know why water was added but people always damped their coke down. It was a temperamental oven and depended on which way the wind was blowing as to how long it took to get hot.

First to make was the teacakes, then meat and potato pies and meat pies. And Elsie always kept a pan going on the cooker, with a good hot bone in, to make gravy. People brought a dish to put their pies in when they wanted gravy on, and though I say it myself, they were the best pies in Cockermouth.

We cooked two roast hams a week and the ham was sold for sixpence a quarter. Scones were a ha'penny, a small white loaf was tuppence ha'penny, and teacakes were a penny each. The ordinary teacakes had lard in them and Elsie's best teacakes or funeral teacakes had butter. We always had a waiting list for these because they kept well. You didn't slice them across, you cut them like bread, downwards.

Everything was to make by hand, there was no machines. For one batch of teacakes we would use about eight pounds of flour and we did two batches a day. Making puff pastry was a hard job, rolling it this way and that, banging it with the rolling pin and adding butter. At that stage it was wrapped in greaseproof paper and put on the back doorstep to cool. I don't think that would pass the hygiene regulations now. Neither would making the ice-cream. Elsie would boil milk the night before to make it 'custardy' and the next day we put it into a container, something like a washing machine. Ice was packed around this container and we had to sit and turn this handle, just like you did with butter, until the ice-cream was ready. I think chocolate eclairs were the most temperamental to make – either they didn't rise or something happened. Then they would go on the shovel and up the flue.

On Saturdays we'd deliver orders to customers. One lady always ordered two blackcurrant tarts and pity help you if you didn't carry them straight, they had to be just so. We also used to open on Good Friday for fresh hot cross buns. People used to like these warm, so we made two batches. Why they couldn't have got them the day before and put them in their ovens, I wouldn't know. Elsie did catering for socials, country dances and the annual police dance. There also used to be a very big police whist drive before Christmas and people came from all over to attend. It was very popular.

Cockermouth Divisional Police Staff, c. 1919

NORAH: We used to get tramps come into the shop and my sister was kind to them. I think they got to know where to come, as Elsie always gave them a loaf of bread. Quite a lot of the folk from the fair came to the shop as well. The fair came to the Main Street in Cockermouth twice a year. They erected everything on the Sunday, so that morning Elsie baked them pies, plate cakes and teacakes. They were very good customers and had money to spend. I used to visit the fair people in their caravans, which were beautiful, and one lady, Mrs Strand, gave me all sorts of nice little bits of pottery.

Next door to Elsie's was a big old-fashioned toy shop where you could buy almost anything: whalebone corsets, kitles [smocks] for men, aprons for maids, wallpaper, everything. Mr Mason who owned the shop also had the agency for the Lakeland Laundry, and the young girl who worked there used an old pram to deliver the laundry to customers. The shop on the other side was Lindsay's the Butcher's, where Elsie got her meat for all the pies, so you knew they would be good.

KATHLEEN: A lot of men worked at the steel works or the coal mines nearer the coast. There was quite a few mines in those days, and in the mornings you could hear the miners going out to work in their clogs. They also had clogs for Sundays, which were polished to death and all carved in a design up the front. They used to shine like glass.

NORAH: At New Year there was a lot of activity, most people going out on to the street at midnight around the Mayo Monument. The Mechanics Band played and people danced. There was a lot of dances in those days, at the Drill Hall, Public Hall, at the little ballroom behind the Appletree, and there was dances in the All Saints Church Rooms. You went first-footing with your friends to different people's houses. We didn't take bottles like they do now, just a piece of coal, and people liked somebody dark to open the door. It was just a lot of fun. You maybe only got a glass of ginger wine and a mince pie and you always fetched friends to your home.

KATHLEEN: In the 1930s Harris Mill that made linen started being altered for Millers Shoe Factory. That's when my dad got a steady job with Border Engineering. Nobody knew what was going on and this was just before the war but they were preparing, they knew something was afoot. Then Dad got a job at Broughton 'Dump' where they employed a lot of people when the war was on. Dad got the highest wage of his life there. If he worked seven days a week he made nearly fifteen pounds. It was an ammunition depot for the navy but everything was well camouflaged and buried. Looking at the place, you wouldn't even know there was anything there.

When the war was starting, the Workhouse that had been empty for years was cleaned out. The authorities got a bunch of women from town to go and scrub it out and I think they were paid two shillings a day. They were at the Workhouse from eight o'clock in the morning until six o'clock at night and the place was filthy. When it was cleaned out, they billeted soldiers there.

NORAH: When the Second World War started my father had died, three brothers were in the forces and one worked at Broughton 'Dump'. That just left my sister and me at home with my mother. I got the word that I'd have to do war work and was told I had a choice between going into 'ammunitions' or the NAAFI. One of my brothers came home on leave and farm work was mentioned. Well, I was keen on gardening and being outside, so I went to work on a farm at Lorton.

I biked the few miles each day to the farm and started at seven in the morning. It wasn't a big farm, only a man and his wife who were very nice and didn't overwork me. My first job was to let the hens out, then milk the cows. The farmer would take the milk down the hill for the Milk Marketing Board to collect and later I would take the horse and bogie [wooden cart] to fetch the milk churns back. Oh, there was always a job to do, thinning turnips, sorting potatoes. When the sheep had been sheared, we would sort the fleeces and sew them into hessian bags. There was a lot of rabbits in that area and a man with a ferret used to come and catch them. Mr Jarman who had a shop in Workington bought the rabbits, as people were desperate for them with the war being on.

KATHLEEN: I was still at Elsie's during the war and rationing made a big difference, you couldn't do the baking you were used to. We got our flour from Harkness's and they would just have to take what they could get but it wasn't nice fine flour. It was horrible, like sawdust, and made your hands burn when you kneaded the dough. I remember we had a waiting list for people wanting the flour bags so they could make pillow cases or coarse aprons. You couldn't get granulated sugar, it was beet sugar, very grey-looking and coarse, not nice at all. Margarine? I think car grease would have tasted better but it was all you could get, there wasn't anything else. When we couldn't get fresh eggs, we started using dried egg yolks that came in big aluminium tins from Canada.

NORAH: You could hear the aeroplanes coming over, on their way up to Scotland, and you could tell they were heavy. They hadn't dropped their loads and when they came back it was a lighter noise and they were travelling a lot faster.

We had two nice little girls, evacuees from Newcastle, staying with us. They got homesick and I suppose things got better over at home and they went back. Years later, one of my sons wrote an article for a Newcastle paper and mentioned Lindsay's good sausages at Cockermouth. Well, a woman who'd been here during the war got in touch with him. He passed the information on to me and I got in touch with this lady. We knew each other, as she had been evacuated to Dr Abraham's, so she came over and stayed for a few days.

Outside Lindsay's Butchers in Cockermouth, c. 1908

There was quite a lot of prisoners of war around. We used to see them every day being taken by lorry to work on the farms. We had a German where I worked who was nice and quiet. You kind of felt sorry for these people more than anything. I mean, they were away from home. But of course some people would feel it because their own lads were away and they weren't well treated, were they?

KATHLEEN: The Germans were good workers but the Italians were entirely different. Oh, they used to strut around with their hats on, just so. It was said that the Italians wore most of their buttons on the backs of their uniform because people saw more of their backs than they ever did of their fronts. But they were all well treated here and got good food.

NORAH: I got married during the war. My husband worked at Silloth Aerodrome when the war was just starting, then he moved to High Duty Alloys. We had our wedding reception at Central Café and Elsie had the day off as she was a bridesmaid. Our honeymoon was spent at Morecambe, just a little boarding house but it was nice. We lived in a flat at Clifton at first and were there when our daughter was born, then moved to Workington. Rationing wasn't too bad. A bit of wheeling and dealing went on and you used to swap things. Older people used to help you out, in fact somebody always helped you out.

KATHLEEN: Talking about Workington, everybody used to go there for the pictures on a Saturday night or to the Opera House where there was some good variety turns. They went by train which was packed and it only cost sixpence return. The trains were very, very good and on Sundays there was a trip to Morecambe for two shillings and sixpence and you could get to Keswick for ninepence.

NORAH: It was a big day when the war finished. People were dancing in the streets, bands were playing and church bells ringing. We managed to rent an old cottage at Cockermouth for three shillings and sixpence a week. It had only one gas light in the living-room, and no lights in the bedrooms or the scullery. There was no electricity or bath and just a sandstone sink in the kitchen which had an earth floor. But eventually, by the time we'd finished with it, the place was lovely.

KATHLEEN: At the end of the war Miss Harkness came into the shop one Monday morning and brought us a bag of white Canadian flour. We almost went nuts. We were eating white bread like there was no tomorrow. Oh, what a treat after all those years.

Years before, when I was at school, we were asked if we wanted Canadian penfriends. I wrote to a girl and after a few letters I found out that her father had been born at Cockermouth and her mother was from Motherby. I didn't meet them until 1948 when the father came over here. He'd been in farm service in the Wigton area until he emigrated in 1912 and his fiancée went out there in 1919, just after the war finished. I had wanted to be a stewardess on a liner but it didn't work out, so I decided I would try Canada and I was told I'd be welcome to stay with them.

It cost me £40 in 1948 to sail from Southampton to New York on the *New Amsterdam*, which was the flagship of the Dutch Shipping Line. From New York, I travelled by train to Sudbury, Ontario, and stayed with my penfriend and her family for thirty-eight years. I got a job in Woolworth's for four years, then I got the chance of a better job in a similar store and was there for twenty-eight years. Being an only daughter, my mother was heartbroken when I left Cockermouth but she realised I wasn't getting anywhere staying here. I promised her I'd come back for a holiday after four years and I came back for six months. After that, I saved hard and came back for a holiday every three years. Eventually my mother had a stroke and, as my two brothers were not married and still lived at home, I felt it was my duty to come back. I've never regretted it. I like Cockermouth and I like Canada where I've still got a mobile home. So for a few months every year, I go back there. The city is about the size of Carlisle and the people are very friendly, almost like they are in the Cockermouth area.

NORAH: It's always been a close-knit community but now families are scattered. It's the younger generation that's gone away, they've gone to colleges, got jobs and simply not come back. It's people's jobs that's taken them away and the communities are going. I never wanted to leave Cockermouth. It's a nice area here and you know everybody. No, I wouldn't leave.

Index